The Princeton Review

Reading and Writing Workout for the SAT

By Geoff Martz
Updated by Mariwyn Curtin

PrincetonReview.com

Random House, Inc. New York

The Princeton Review, Inc.
111 Speen Street, Suite 550
Framingham, MA 01701
E-mail: editorialsupport@review.com

ISBN 978-0-375-42832-6
ISSN 1551-6423

Editor: Liz Rutzel
Production Editor: Kathy G. Carter
Production Coordinator: Deborah A. Silvestrini

Printed in the United States of America
on partially recycled paper.

10 9 8 7 6 5 4 3 2 1

Second Edition

Editorial
Seamus Mullarkey, Editorial Director
Laura Braswell, Senior Editor
Heather Brady, Editor
Selena Coppock, Editor

Random House Publishing Team
Tom Russell, Publisher
Nicole Benhabib, Publishing Manager
Ellen L. Reed, Production Manager
Alison Stoltzfus, Associate Managing Editor

ACKNOWLEDGMENTS

Thanks to Lee Elliott, Kristin Fayne-Mulroy, Chris Kensler, Marcia Lerner, Mia Barron, Jeannie Yoon, Jane Lacher, and all the Princeton Review teachers whose ingenuity and hard work made this book possible. For additional production and editing help, thanks to Doug Pierce, Suzanne Markert, Russell Kahn, Maria Dente, Patricia Dublin, Stephanie J. Martin, Jeff Rubenstein, Andrea Paykin, Andy Lutz, Cynthia Brantley, Julian Ham, Andrew Dunn, Debbie Guest, Clayton Harding, Kathleen Standard, Christopher D. Scott, Jefferson Nichols, Joe Cavallaro, Sara Kane, Ramsey Silberberg, Matthew Clark, and Carol Slominski.

Thanks to Mariwyn Curtin and Patrick Tyrrell for their work on this revision. Special thanks to Adam Robinson, who conceived of and perfected the Joe Bloggs approach to standardized tests, and many other techniques in this book.

ABOUT THE AUTHOR

After attending Dartmouth and Columbia, Geoff Martz joined The Princeton Review as a teacher and writer. He is the author or co-author of *Cracking the GMAT, Cracking the ACT, Cracking the GED, Paying for College, How to Survive Without Your Parents' Money,* and the CD-ROM software program *Inside the SAT.*

CONTENTS

PART I

Orientation

Introduction

READ THIS STUFF FIRST

Wouldn't it be great if all the problems on the Grammar sections of the SAT looked like this?

> **2.** The armadillo, like the sloth and the anteater, <u>have teeth that lack both enamel and roots</u>.
>
> (A) have teeth that lack both enamel and roots
> (B) has teeth that lack both enamel and roots **(Hey you! Pick this one!)**
> (C) having teeth that are lacking in both enamel and roots
> (D) all have teeth that lack both enamel and roots
> (E) each with teeth that are lacking enamel and roots

> **16.** <u>During</u> the early years of WWII, it <u>seemed</u> as
>   A   B
>
> though <u>Germany's army</u> would
>   C
>
> <u>prove stronger than any other nation.</u> <u>No error</u>
>   D   E

This one's too hard. Just put down (D). We know you're smart.

—Love, ETS

Only in our dreams is ETS (Educational Testing Service, the company that writes the SAT) this benevolent. But believe it or not, the ETS test writers *do* provide clues (sometimes on purpose, sometimes inadvertently) to every single question. This workbook will show you how to find those clues so that you can get every point you deserve on the Critical Reading and Writing parts of the test—and maybe even a few that you don't.

In the section on Sentence Completions, we'll show you how to spot the clues ETS has left for you. In the section on Critical Reading passages, we'll demonstrate how to find the important information in a passage—and skip the rest. In the Grammar section we'll reveal exactly what types of errors to keep your eyes peeled for. And the Writing section will help you write the perfect ETS essay.

The techniques we'll show you are not based solely on our opinions or private theories. They've been proven by the students who have taken our SAT course over the past 20-plus years.

But let's start at the beginning.

Verbal Skills = $^2/_3$ of the SAT

The SAT has nine scored sections, and the majority of them test your verbal skills. There are three sections of Critical Reading and a three-part Writing section, for a total of six sections that test some kind of verbal skills. This book will help you with what's tested in the Critical Reading and Writing sections, including sentence completions, critical reading, grammar, and essay writing.

The first thing you'll see on the SAT is the Writing section's essay, which will give you 25 minutes to write an essay. The Writing section also includes one 25-minute section and one 10-minute section, which test your grammar and writing skills by asking you to identify grammatical errors and improve sentences and paragraphs.

In the Critical Reading section, two 25-minute multiple-choice sections will test what ETS calls your "critical reading" abilities with sentence completions and short and long reading passages. An additional 20-minute section will have sentence completion and long reading passages, but no short reading.

Here's what the breakdown looks like:

1. One 25-minute Writing section made up of
   - 1 essay question

2. One 25-minute Writing section made up of
   - error identification questions
   - improving sentences questions
   - improving paragraphs questions

3. One 10-minute Writing section made up of only improving sentences

4. Two 25-minute Critical Reading sections made up of
   - sentence completion questions
   - short reading comprehension questions
   - long reading comprehension questions

5. One 20-minute Critical Reading section made up of
   - sentence completion questions
   - long reading comprehension questions

In this book, you will find two practice test sections: Reading Comprehension and Grammar. These practice sections are similar to what you will find on the SAT. Take them timed, just as you would on test day.

HOW THE SAT IS SCORED

There are a total of 67 Critical Reading questions on the SAT. Each correct answer earns you one "raw point." For each incorrect answer, ETS subtracts a quarter of a raw point. Your total raw score is then converted to a 200- to 800-point scale. Your Critical Reading SAT score (along with your Math and Writing SAT scores) will be sent to you (and the colleges to which you are applying) about five weeks after you take the test. These scores are reported in 10-point increments. In other words, you can get a 510 or a 520, but never a 514. The Writing sections of the test include 49 multiple-choice questions and one essay. The multiple-choice questions in the Writing section will be graded similarly to those in the Critical Reading section, with each correct answer earning you one raw point and each incorrect answer losing you a quarter of a raw point. Your essay will be scored by two separate graders for a combined raw score of 2–12 points. Through a magic conversion formula, the essay score will count for 30 percent of your score on the Writing section.

WHAT IS CONSIDERED A GOOD SCORE ON THE SAT?

The average Critical Reading SAT score is approximately 500. The average Writing score is a little lower, at 492 for the class of 2010. If you want to find out what scores are required at particular colleges, you should consult one of the college guides found in bookstores (we are partial to *The Princeton Review Guide to the Best 373 Colleges*). Bear in mind that the colleges report either average or median scores, which means that many students with SAT scores well below the published average or median scores are accepted by those colleges.

In addition, colleges consider several factors when making admissions decisions. Your SAT score is a big factor, but not the only one.

HOW YOU TRULY SCORE HIGHER ON THE SAT

The real way to improve your SAT Critical Reading and Writing scores is to answer more questions correctly. However, many students become frustrated on the Critical Reading and Writing portions of the SAT because they are not sure why the answer they pick isn't the "best" answer. This book will show you exactly how to find what ETS considers the best answer and thus help you increase the number of questions you answer correctly.

IMPROVING YOUR VOCABULARY

From a long-term perspective, a good vocabulary will win you good grades in college, will help you find jobs and gain promotions, and may even impress your friends.

And from a long-term perspective, the best way to build a better vocabulary is to read. A lot.

We heartily recommend this course of action, but we also recognize that if you have only one month until the SAT, there isn't time to read the collected works of Thackeray or even of Dave Barry.

However, from a short-term perspective, it turns out that learning a very small number of carefully selected words can really increase your Critical Reading SAT score. We fed a computer all the words that have appeared on the old Verbal SAT over a ten-year span; it generated a list of roughly 250 words that are likely to continue to appear on the Critical Reading sections of the SAT. These words (called the Hit Parade), along with the techniques for memorizing them, make up the bulk of the vocabulary section of this book. The words are arranged in small, useful groups, by situations.

Before you go on, turn to the Vocabulary section and think about a feasible schedule to memorize the Hit Parade words in the time remaining before you take the SAT. We promise you won't regret it.

A NOTE TO OUR STUDENTS

This book contains the most up-to-date information on the SAT available as of press time. We at The Princeton Review want to make sure you have access to the most accurate and current information possible. Please be sure to visit our website at **PrincetonReview.com** for periodic updates on all things related to the SAT. And while you're there, don't forget to check out all the cool resources we have to help you with every part of the college admissions process. You should also check out www.CollegeBoard.com for updates straight from the test-writers themselves.

Now let's talk strategies.

1
Strategies

THE ART OF ELIMINATION

Take a look at the following sentence completion—in an unusual format that you will never see on the SAT:

> 7. Bien qu'il soit trés vieux, il parait
>   toujours -------.

You may think the unusual thing about this question is that it's in French, (okay, we admit that's pretty unusual), but the *really* unusual thing about this question—the thing that makes it different from every question on the Critical Reading and Writing parts of SAT—is that it's not in a multiple-choice format.

You might be saying, "Who cares? Multiple-choice or fill-in—I can't answer it anyway. It's in *French*."

As it stands right now, unless you speak French, you have no idea what word goes in the blank (and by the way, there are no questions in French on the SAT). But let's turn this question into a multiple-choice question and see if you can figure out the answer now:

> 7. Bien qu'il soit trés vieux, il parait
>   toujours -------.
>
> (A) earnest
> (B) timid
> (C) exhausted
> (D) jeune
> (E) elated

Cross out all of the answers you know must not fit the sentence. All of a sudden, this problem doesn't seem so hard, does it? Multiple-choice tests (in *any* language) always give test takers an inherent advantage: There are only a finite number of possible choices. And while you might not know the correct answer to this problem, you know that four choices are probably wrong. (The correct answer is choice D.)

ELIMINATING WRONG ANSWERS

There will be many problems on the SAT for which you will be able to identify the correct answer (particularly if you learn the Hit Parade words). However, there will be others about which you will not be sure. Should you simply skip these problems? Not if you can eliminate wrong answers. Wrong answers are often easier to spot than right answers. Sometimes they just sound wrong in the context of the sentence. Other times they are logically impossible. While you will rarely be able to eliminate all the incorrect answer choices on an SAT question, it is often possible to eliminate two or three. And each time you eliminate an answer choice, your odds of guessing correctly get better.

GUESSING IS GOOD

Every time you get a question right, ETS gives you one raw point. To discourage you from guessing at random, ETS deducts a quarter of a raw point from your score for each incorrect answer you choose. ETS calls this a guessing penalty, but in fact, it is not a penalty at all. Let's say you guess at random on five questions. The laws of probability say that you will get one of these questions right (so ETS gives you 1 raw point) and the other four wrong (so ETS takes away 4 quarter points). In other words, you will come out dead even. This means that guessing completely at random on the SAT won't help your score, and it won't hurt your score.

Ah, but who said anything about guessing at random?

Let's look at the same question again, but with slightly different answers:

7. Bien qu'il soit trés vieux, il parait
toujours -------.

    (A) earnest
    (B) timid
    (C) sérieux
    (D) jeune
    (E) elated

This time, even without knowing French, you can eliminate three of the answer choices. This gives you a fifty-fifty guess—much better than random guessing. It turns out that if you can eliminate even one answer choice, then it is in your interest to guess. You will find that our techniques for sentence completions will help you eliminate answer choices, even when you don't know the words.

ORDER OF DIFFICULTY

Sentence completion questions on the SAT are arranged in order of difficulty. There will be five sentence completions in one of the two 25-minute Critical Reading sections and eight in the other. The 20-minute section has six sentence completions. Within each section, these questions are arranged so that the easiest question comes first, the most difficult question comes last, and the others are arranged in ascending order of difficulty in between.

The critical reading questions are *not* arranged in order of difficulty. Instead, these questions appear in the order in which the information that is required to answer them is found in the passage.

The difficulty level of a question reflects the percentage of test takers who usually get that question correct. Depending on which words you happen to know, a question that is considered "hard" might be easy for you, while you might find an "easy" question to be difficult if it contains unfamiliar words. Nevertheless, it is a good idea to think of each group of questions in sentence completions as being in thirds. The first third is relatively easy. The second third is medium. The last third contains the questions that most people find difficult.

Easy Questions Have Easy Answers—
Hard Questions Have Hard Answers

The order of difficulty is important because it will prevent you from overthinking. An easy question is supposed to have an easy answer. A difficult problem will have a difficult answer. If you find yourself wrestling with the first sentence completion, you are probably looking for subtlety that isn't there. If you find yourself picking the first choice that comes into your head on the last sentence completion, you may want to think it through again.

Distractors

The ETS test writers think constantly about the order of difficulty because they are obsessed with making sure that students correctly answer only the questions that they "deserve to get right." The average test taker is supposed to get all of the easy questions right, some of the medium questions right, and all of the difficult questions wrong.

There's only one potential problem here: What if the average test taker were to guess correctly on a difficult question? The ETS test writers hate this idea so much that in the difficult third of a group of questions they sometimes include distractor answers that are designed to trick the average test taker.

JOE BLOGGS

Joe Bloggs is our name for the average test taker. He's the guy who always writes down the first answer that comes into his head. Because the first answer that comes into his head is correct on easy questions, he gets all the easy questions correct. And because the first answer that comes into his head is *sometimes* correct on medium questions, he gets *some* of the medium questions correct. But the first answer that enters Joe's mind is always wrong on difficult questions, so Joe Bloggs gets all of the difficult questions wrong.

To make sure this remains true, the ETS test writers will occasionally help Joe to make the *wrong* decision. Let's see how this works. Here's a sentence completion from the last and hardest third of a group of sentence completions:

8. Despite the ------- of evidence against the
   suspect, the jury found him guilty on all counts.

   (A) preponderance
   (B) weight
   (C) paucity
   (D) deliberation
   (E) objection

DON'T BE LIKE JOE

We're going to talk about how to approach sentence completions later in the book, so don't worry if you're not sure how to get the correct answer. For now, let's discuss how Joe tries to tackle this problem (and if Joe's method is similar to yours, that's okay; there's a little of Joe Bloggs in each of us). When Joe reads a sentence completion, he likes to pick an answer that sounds good in the sentence. Usually the word that sounds good to Joe reminds him of the other words in the sentence. Do any of the answers seem like something he'd like?

If you said choice D or E, you've got the idea. When Joe isn't entirely sure of what the sentence is saying, he's likely to pick a choice that feels right to him. Because this sentence has a courtroom theme, Joe might go with "objection" or "deliberation," two words he's probably heard on popular TV court shows. Of course, ETS knows this, and both of those choices are wrong. The best answer is choice C.

Remember, though, that the only time you need to look out for distractor answers is in the last third of a group of questions (the hardest questions in the set).

PACING

Each of the 25-minute Critical Reading sections will contain three types of questions: sentence completions, short reading, and critical reading. The 20-minute section has only sentence completion and long-passage critical reading questions. In general, the reading questions take longer to do than the sentence completions. If you have a good vocabulary, tackle the sentence completions first and then move on to the reading questions. If vocabulary isn't your strong point, spend more time with the reading questions (but be sure to study the vocabulary in Chapter 7; the better your vocabulary, the better your reading level—and your score). Use whatever time you have left to deal with the sentence completions.

The 35-question Writing section will contain questions broken down into three types: error identification, improving sentences, and improving paragraphs. As with sentence completions, error identification and improving sentences questions are arranged roughly in order of difficulty. The error identification questions generally take the least amount of time and should be done first. After you've finished them, or if the last third of error identifications gets tough, move on to the improving sentences. The order of difficulty starts over with easy questions at the beginning of both question types. Save the improving paragraphs questions for last. There is no order of difficulty for improving paragraphs—most are of medium difficulty.

The 10-minute Writing section is always Section 10. It has only 14 questions, all of which are improving sentences questions.

You don't have to answer every question on the test to get a good score; it's okay if you skip questions as you work. However, as you learn the strategies in this book, you'll see that on most questions you will be able to eliminate at least one answer. In that case, it pays to be aggressive and guess. The higher you aim to score, the more questions you'll need to attempt.

PACE YOURSELF

While the following pacing charts for Critical Reading and Writing give you an idea of how many questions to do, they don't tell you *which* questions to do. If the chart tells you to do 16 questions in a particular section, that doesn't necessarily mean you should do the *first* 16. Focus on first doing the medium and easy questions; then work on the more difficult ones if you need more questions to reach your target score.

In Critical Reading, only the arrangements of sentence completion questions follow an order of difficulty.

In Writing, the improving sentences have an order of difficulty, and the error identifications start with easy questions and a fresh order of difficulty even though they start at question 12. There is no order of difficulty for improving passages.

These pacing charts are only an approximate guide. ETS has a way of changing things at the last minute, so don't worry if there are slightly more or fewer questions in each section when you take the test. Just hold your pacing to your score level, and you'll do fine.

CRITICAL READING PACING CHART

To get: (scaled score)	You Need: (raw points)	Answer this many questions			Total # of questions to attempt
		24 question section	24 question section	19 question section	
300	5	6	6	3	15
350	9	8	8	4	20
400	14	11	11	8	30
450	21	14	14	10	38
500	29	16	16	11	43
550	38	19	19	13	51
600	46	22	22	16	60
650	53	23	23	17	63
700	59	23	23	18	64
750	63	all	all	all	67
800	67	all	all	all	67

WRITING

The scaled Writing section score (200–800) is derived from two components: the essay score and the multiple-choice grammar score (which is scaled from 20–80). Two different people grade your essay, and each gives it a score on a scale of 1–6. The sum of these two scores is weighted to make the essay score worth approximately 30 percent of the total score; then the result is added to your grammar raw score to get your final writing score.

WRITING SCORES

If your scaled grammar score is ...	Depending on your essay score, your writing score will range from
20	200–320
25	200–370
30	250–420
35	280–460
40	330–500
45	360–540
50	410–590
55	450–630
60	490–670
65	530–710
70	570–750
75	620–800
80	680–800

The following pacing chart will help you decide how many multiple-choice grammar questions to do.

GRAMMAR PACING CHART

To get: (scaled score)	You Need: (raw points)	Answer this many questions		
		35 question section	14 question section	Total # of questions to attempt
35	5	10	5	15
40	11	13	7	20
45	17	18	8	26
50	22	22	9	31
55	27	26	10	36
60	31	27	11	38
65	36	31	all	45
70	40	all	all	49
75	44	all	all	49
80	49	all	all	49

WHAT IS THE PRINCETON REVIEW?

The Princeton Review is the nation's fastest-growing test-preparation company. We give courses in more than 500 locations and online, and publish best-selling books and software to get students ready for this test. We also prepare students for the PSAT/NMSQT, ACT, GRE, GMAT, LSAT, MCAT, and other standardized tests.

The Princeton Review's techniques are unique and powerful. We developed them after spending countless hours scrutinizing real SATs, analyzing them with computers, and proving our theories with real students. Our methods have been widely imitated, but no one else achieves our score improvements.

This book is based on our extensive experience in the classroom. Our techniques for cracking the SAT will help you improve your SAT scores by teaching you to

1. think like the test writers at ETS

2. take full advantage of the limited time allowed

3. find the answers to questions you don't understand by guessing intelligently

4. avoid the traps that ETS has laid for you (and use those traps to your advantage)

EVEN ETS KNOWS OUR TECHNIQUES WORK

ETS has spent a great deal of time and money over the years trying to persuade people that the SAT can't be cracked. At the same time, ETS has struggled to find ways of changing the SAT so that The Princeton Review won't be able to crack it—in effect acknowledging what our students have known all along, which is that our techniques really do work. Despite ETS's efforts, the SAT remains highly vulnerable to our techniques. In fact, the current format of the test is more coachable than ever.

TAKING CHARGE

So much in life is outside of our control, and sometimes it's hard not to let ourselves get pushed around. The process of taking the SAT can sometimes feel like that. They tell you when to show up. They tell you where to sit. They tell you when to begin and when to stop. They even tell you the *number* of the pencil that you must bring with you.

In the face of all this control, it's easy to think that there is nothing you can do to take charge, but in fact *nothing could be further from the truth.*

The way you take charge is by preparing ahead of time, by learning the strategies and techniques we're going to show you in the chapters ahead, by learning what is actually going to be on the test, by being aggressive, and by eliminating wrong answers.

And the most important way you can take charge is by keeping your sense of perspective. It's only a test.

PART ◆ II
Critical Reading

2

Sentence Completions

SENTENCE COMPLETIONS

Every Critical Reading section of the SAT begins with a group of sentence completion questions. There are five or eight sentence completions in the 25-minute sections and six in the 20-minute section for a total of 19 sentence completions per test. The questions within each section are arranged in order of difficulty. Because of the terrific elimination techniques we will show you below, you will probably be able to take a good guess on all of the sentence completions—even when you don't know the definitions of some of the words.

Let's begin by looking at an example of a sentence completion that unfortunately you will *never* see on the SAT:

   1. Jane ------- the DVD player.

      (A) installed
      (B) dropped
      (C) programmed
      (D) stole
      (E) shot

Why won't you ever see this question on the SAT? Because the way this sentence is written, *all* of the answer choices would be correct. What? You didn't think choice E could be right? Well, how about this:

   2. After trying unsuccessfully to program it for
      three hours, Jane ------- the DVD player.

      (A) installed
      (B) dropped
      (C) programmed
      (D) stole
      (E) shot

To make sure that only one answer choice is correct per question, ETS always provides you with a clue (such as the one you just saw above) within the sentence itself. The clause "after trying unsuccessfully to program it for three hours..." gives away Jane's state of mind, and helps us to choose the correct answer. Let's look at the same sentence written several different ways. See if you can supply the missing word:

   3. While trying to lift the DVD player, Jane
      ------- it.

      (A) installed
      (B) dropped
      (C) programmed
      (D) stole
      (E) shot

4. Because she wanted to tape a program when she wasn't home, Jane ------- the DVD player.

(A) installed
(B) dropped
(C) programmed
(D) stole
(E) shot

5. After breaking into the house through the window, Jane ------- the DVD player.

(A) installed
(B) dropped
(C) programmed
(D) stole
(E) shot

(Answers: 2. E, 3. B, 4. C, 5. D)

Each of these sentences contained a clue that led you to the correct answer. While the real SAT sentence completion questions are a bit more difficult, the same principle always applies. The way to answer a sentence completion question is to look for the clue that *must* be there, in order for the question to have one answer that is better than the others.

THE CLUE
Take a look at the following two questions.

1. The woman told the man, "You're very -------."

(A) handsome
(B) sick
(C) smart
(D) foolish
(E) good

2. The doctor told the man, "You're very -------."

(A) handsome
(B) sick
(C) happy
(D) foolish
(E) good

Which of these two questions actually has a single correct answer, question 1 or 2?

If you said question 2, you're right. In question 2, there's only one possible answer: choice B. The words are the clue. Every sentence completion has a the clue: a key word or phrase that tells you what kind of word you need to fill in the blank.

> Always be on the lookout for the clue: the word or phrase that ETS gives you to help anticipate the word that will best fit in the blank.

Here's an example.

5. So ------- was the young boy's behavior that his teachers decided to give him a gold star.

    (A) exemplary
    (B) unruly
    (C) arrogant
    (D) radical
    (E) imaginative

THE PRINCETON REVIEW METHOD

Step One   Cover up the answer choices. ETS wants several of these choices to appear likely if you haven't found the clue. For example, if you were to look straight at the answer choices in this question, your eye might be caught by choice B, "unruly," or choice C, "arrogant"—just because those are often words a teacher might use to describe a student's behavior.

> Cover up the answer choices until you have found the clue in the sentence.

Step Two   Look for the clue. Have you spotted it? In this case, the clue was in the very last words of the sentence: "gold star." If these teachers want to give a student a "gold star," what word would you use to describe his behavior? Try making up your own word to fit the blank. If you chose a word like "good" or "excellent" or "flawless," you were right on track.

Step Three   Look at the answer choices and see which one comes closest to the word you think should go in the blank. Eliminate any that are definitely wrong. In this case, eliminate choices B and C because they are almost exactly the opposite of the word you are looking for. *Physically cross off these two choices.* Would "radical" behavior necessarily lead to a gold star? Not really, so cross off choice D as well.

Step Four   If you still have choices left, guess among the remaining possibilities. In this example, you are down to choice A, "exemplary," and choice E, "imaginative." If you know the meaning of the word exemplary (one of the words on the Hit Parade), then your choice is easy. But let's say for a moment that you aren't sure. The first thing to do in this situation is not to panic—you are down to a fifty-fifty guess, which is already pretty good. Now, if you don't know the meaning of the word, of course you can't cross it off. So look instead at the other word. Do teachers reward imagination? They might. But do they reward imaginative *behavior*? What exactly would imaginative behavior look like? Mostly, teachers like imagination only when it is in a composition or a finger painting. It might be a little threatening if it exhibited itself in *behavior*.

You're down to choices A and E. Guess. If you picked choice A, you are 10 points ahead. Exemplary means "ideal," or "worthy of imitation."

QUICK QUIZ #1

Begin by covering up the answer choices. Try to spot the clue, and come up with your own idea of what the missing word might be. Then go to the answer choices and eliminate wrong answers. Finally, pick the answer you think is correct.

1. By means of her ------- demeanor, Lucy Ortiz calmly worked her way up to the position of head salesperson at the chaotic brokerage house.

   (A) cunning
   (B) serene
   (C) frenzied
   (D) gullible
   (E) unstable

2. Large facial features have often been the mark of successful people; many of our recent presidents have had ------- noses.

   (A) insignificant
   (B) typical
   (C) unusual
   (D) prominent
   (E) subtle

3. Sightings of the tern, a small marsh bird once considered endangered, are becoming almost -------.

   (A) commonplace
   (B) erratic
   (C) precarious
   (D) virtuous
   (E) uniform

4. Glaucoma, a serious eye ailment that can lead to blindness, is almost always ------- if it is caught in its early stages.

   (A) fatal
   (B) congenital
   (C) unethical
   (D) verifiable
   (E) treatable

5. The consummate opera singer Kathleen Battle has long had the reputation for being a difficult, even -------, personality.

   (A) entertaining
   (B) malleable
   (C) contentious
   (D) deliberate
   (E) bland

1 ⊂A⊃ ⊂B⊃ ⊂C⊃ ⊂D⊃ ⊂E⊃
2 ⊂A⊃ ⊂B⊃ ⊂C⊃ ⊂D⊃ ⊂E⊃
3 ⊂A⊃ ⊂B⊃ ⊂C⊃ ⊂D⊃ ⊂E⊃
4 ⊂A⊃ ⊂B⊃ ⊂C⊃ ⊂D⊃ ⊂E⊃
5 ⊂A⊃ ⊂B⊃ ⊂C⊃ ⊂D⊃ ⊂E⊃

Answers and Explanations: Quick Quiz #1

1. **B** The clue here is the word "calmly." You might be thrown off by the "chaotic" atmosphere at the brokerage house and think that Lucy must be pretty chaotic herself in order to fit in. However, the sentence makes clear that it is her calmness that allows her to succeed in the hectic business. If you came up with a word like "evenness" or "placid" or "tranquil," you were right on the money.

   Looking at the answer choices, you can eliminate everything but choice B, "serene."

2. **D** The clue in this sentence is the word "large" referring to the facial features of successful people. What kind of noses, then, according to this sentence, would you expect to find on recent presidents? If you chose words like "huge" or "big" or "gigantic," you were right on the money.

   Choice C is tempting, because a really large nose would be kind of unusual, but choice D is better because it clearly signifies "large."

3. **A** The clue here is the phrase "once considered endangered." If the bird was *once* considered endangered, then it isn't *now*. What word would describe sightings of this bird, which is no longer in danger of becoming extinct? If you chose a word like "mundane" or "everyday" or "routine," then you are doing just fine. Both choices B and C would be good possibilities if the bird were still endangered, but because it is not, eliminate them. Choice E might seem tempting at first, but the secondary definition of uniform (not what a boy scout wears) is "identical or alike." The best answer is "commonplace."

4. **E** Both choices A, "fatal," and B, "congenital" (meaning "from birth"), are often used to describe diseases, but neither is the right answer this time. The clue in this sentence is the phrase "if it is caught in its early stages." What word would you use to describe a disease discovered in its early stages? If you came up with "curable" or "correctable" or "relievable," you were right on track. The best answer here is choice E, "treatable."

5. **C** The clue in this sentence is the phrase "a difficult, even -------
   personality." Whenever you see this format, (a -------, even -------),
   the second word is almost always a more extreme version of the first word. (For example, "The weather was gray, even gloomy.") Therefore, what you are looking for in this sentence is a more extreme version of the word "difficult." If you came up with words like "troublesome" or "argumentative," you were right on the money. The best answer is choice C, "contentious" (meaning "quarrelsome").

TRIGGER WORDS

Certain words reveal a lot about the structure of a sentence. We call these words "trigger words." Trigger words work with the clue to help you figure out the meaning of the word in the blank. Take a look at the following sentence:

You're beautiful, *but* you're . . .

What kind of word would go in the blank? Something negative, such as "rude" or "unpleasant."

The word "but" in the sentence above tells you all you have to know: Whatever has been expressed in the first half of the sentence is about to be contradicted in the second half. Words like "but" are structural clues to the meaning of the sentence.

Here's a list of the trigger words that signal a contradiction:	
but	however
although	even though
despite	though
rather	on the contrary
yet	in contrast

On the other hand, there are other words that signal that the second half of the sentence will continue in the *same* general direction as the first half. Here's an example:

You're beautiful, *and* you're very. . .

What kind of word go in this blank? Something positive, such as "smart" or "sweet."

The word "and" in the sentence above tells you what kind of word will go in the blank: Whatever thought has been expressed in the first half of the sentence (something positive) will be *continued* or amplified in the second half (something positive). Words like "and," when they appear in a sentence completion problem, are also structural clues to the meaning of the sentence.

Here's a list of the words that signal a continuation or an amplification of the direction in a sentence:

and	in fact
not only	but also
because	indeed, even

Always circle these trigger words whenever you see them. These words, along with the clue, will help you to figure out the meaning of the blank.

QUICK QUIZ #2

Begin by covering up the answer choices. Try to come up with the missing word using trigger words and the clue. Then go to the answer choices and eliminate wrong answers. Finally, pick the answer you think is correct.

1. Despite government efforts at population control, the number of people in China continues to ------- rapidly.

   (A) decline
   (B) increase
   (C) fluctuate
   (D) stabilize
   (E) deploy

2. Archeologists believed until recently that the ancient Mayans lived exclusively in permanent settlements, but new evidence suggests that some of the Mayans made seasonal -------.

   (A) migrations
   (B) resolutions
   (C) renunciations
   (D) sanctions
   (E) speculations

3. During the height of the civil war, the diplomatic efforts by Sweden to enforce a cease-fire were regarded by both sides not only with ------- but also with derision.

   (A) delight
   (B) reverence
   (C) scorn
   (D) vigor
   (E) yearning

4. The museum has many fine paintings by van Gogh, including his ------- and haunted self-portrait with the bandaged ear.

   (A) tranquil
   (B) haughty
   (C) colorful
   (D) repetitive
   (E) anguished

5. Although many of the people at the party accepted John's account of the evening's events, Jason believed it to be -------.

   (A) generous
   (B) credible
   (C) unusual
   (D) inferior
   (E) apocryphal

1 ⊂A⊃ ⊂B⊃ ⊂C⊃ ⊂D⊃ ⊂E⊃
2 ⊂A⊃ ⊂B⊃ ⊂C⊃ ⊂D⊃ ⊂E⊃
3 ⊂A⊃ ⊂B⊃ ⊂C⊃ ⊂D⊃ ⊂E⊃
4 ⊂A⊃ ⊂B⊃ ⊂C⊃ ⊂D⊃ ⊂E⊃
5 ⊂A⊃ ⊂B⊃ ⊂C⊃ ⊂D⊃ ⊂E⊃

Answers and Explanations: Quick Quiz #2

1. **B** The trigger word in this sentence ("despite") signifies that the second half of the sentence is going to contradict the first. Because the first half refers to population *control*, what do you think the number of people is going to continue to do? If you said "multiply" or "grow" you were right. The correct answer is choice B.

2. **A** The trigger word ("but") signifies that the new evidence is going to contradict what archeologists believed until recently. The missing word should mean something like "trips" or "movements." The best answer is choice A.

3. **C** The construction "not only...but also..." means that the word in front of the "but also" must be similar to the word after the "but also." Thus, the missing word must resemble the word "derision." If you know the meaning of "derision" then the choice is fairly clear. However, let's say for a moment that you aren't sure. Have you at least got a feeling about the word? Does it sound positive or negative? If you said "negative," you were right. Which of the answer choices also sounds negative? The word that is most similar to "derision" (meaning "mockery") is choice C, "scorn."

4. **E** An "and" injected in between two adjectives usually means the two adjectives must be somewhat similar. In this case, you don't know the first word describing a painting by van Gogh, but it must be similar to the second word, "haunted." Which choices can you eliminate? It's pretty easy to eliminate choices A, C, and D. "Haughty" (meaning "arrogant or condescending") doesn't exactly seem similar to "haunted." The correct answer is choice E.

5. **E** The trigger in this sentence is the word "although," which signals that the second half of the sentence will contradict the first. In the first half, you are told that many people accepted John's story as true. In the second half, you are supposed to learn that Jason did not. If you chose a word like "a lie" then you were right on track. Go through the answer choices. If Jason believed John's story was choice A, "generous," would that contradict the general belief that his story was true? Not really. If Jason believed John's story was choice B, "credible" (meaning "believable"), would that contradict the general belief? Actually, just the reverse. If Jason believed John's story was choice C, "unusual," would that contradict the general belief? Maybe. Hold on to that one and look at the other two. If Jason believed John's story was choice D, "inferior," would that contradict the general belief? Maybe. Hold on to that one as well. If Jason believed John's story was choice E, "apocryphal" (meaning "fictional or made up"), would that contradict the general belief? You bet. The best answer to this fairly difficult problem is choice E.

DEGREE OF DIFFICULTY

Because all sentence completions are arranged in order of difficulty, you can frequently learn important things about a missing word simply by the question number, which tells you how hard the question is. The first two or three sentence completions in a group are supposed to be relatively easy. This means that the correct answer to one of these questions should be a relatively easy vocabulary word as well. The middle three or four sentence completions are supposed to be of medium difficulty. The correct answers to these questions will be words of medium difficulty. The last two or three sentence completions are supposed to be quite difficult. The correct answers to these questions will be quite tough vocabulary words, or medium words that have secondary meanings.

If you don't know some of the words in a difficult sentence completion question, you might think that you would have to leave it blank—but that is not necessarily the case. Let's see how you could use order of difficulty to eliminate answer choices on the last three sentence completions. What follows are only the answer choices from one of the last three sentence completion questions of an actual SAT. Based on the fact that tough questions tend to have tough answers, which of these choices are *unlikely* to be the correct answer?

(A) cosmopolitan
(B) wavering
(C) plucky
(D) vindictive
(E) bellicose

Put it this way: Which of these words would be familiar to just about anyone? "Cosmopolitan" is a fairly common word, as are "wavering" and "plucky." Therefore, if you were simply to guess the answer to this difficult sentence completion without the benefit of the sentence itself, you would be tempted to pick either choice D, "vindictive," or choice E, "bellicose." The correct answer to this real ETS question turns out to be choice E. Will this work every time? Of course not. This is merely a last-ditch guessing strategy if you don't understand enough of the sentence to be able to search for contextual clues.

> **Remember that the answers to difficult sentence completions tend to use difficult vocabulary words.**

The real value of this strategy comes when you have already eliminated several answer choices by other means: You're down to two, and you can't figure out which one is the answer. If the question is one of the last three sentence completions, you should pick the answer choice containing the more difficult word.

QUICK QUIZ #3

Pretend that the following are answer choices for the last, and therefore hardest, sentence completions in a set of eight. As a last-ditch guessing strategy, eliminate answer choices that seem too easy to be the correct answers to difficult problems.

1. (A) supplied
    (B) tainted
    (C) betrayed
    (D) corrected
    (E) increased

2. (A) complexity
    (B) uniqueness
    (C) exorbitance
    (D) paucity
    (E) fragility

3. (A) **already eliminated**
    (B) indifference .. legitimate
    (C) **already eliminated**
    (D) immunity .. hyperbolic
    (E) **already eliminated**

1 ⊂A⊃ ⊂B⊃ ⊂C⊃ ⊂D⊃ ⊂E⊃
2 ⊂A⊃ ⊂B⊃ ⊂C⊃ ⊂D⊃ ⊂E⊃
3 ⊂A⊃ ⊂B⊃ ⊂C⊃ ⊂D⊃ ⊂E⊃

ANSWERS AND EXPLANATIONS: QUICK QUIZ #3

1. **B** Eliminate choices A, D, and E. The correct answer to this real ETS question is choice B.

2. **D** Eliminate choices A and B. The correct answer to this real ETS question is choice D.

3. **D** Imagine that you have already eliminated A, C, and E through context clues, but you can't decide between choices B and D. Do either of them seem too easy to be the answer to a tough question? Eliminate choice B. The correct answer to this real ETS question is choice D.

IS A MISSING WORD POSITIVE OR NEGATIVE?

While sometimes you may not be sure *exactly* what word would fit the blank, you may be able to get a feeling for whether the missing word should be generally positive or generally negative.

> 6. When Lattitia Douglas was ------- by the railroad company in 1903, it represented a personal victory for her.

While you may not know exactly what word ETS chose for this blank, you can be pretty sure it was a positive word based on the clue ("a victory").

Just as important, when you look at the answer choices, you may not know the meaning of every word, but you may have a "feeling" about certain words even without knowing their exact definitions. Here are the answer choices to this question:

> (A) censured
> (B) lauded
> (C) rebuked
> (D) rebutted
> (E) undermined

As you go through the Vocabulary section of this book, you will probably be amazed at how often the words you've just learned come up on real SAT practice sections. Because we show you only words that appear again and again on the test, this is really not all that amazing. However, for every new word that you learn, there will be several whose meanings you haven't quite memorized yet—but that you have *seen* several times before.

> **NOTE: You can decide that a word is negative or positive only if you have seen it before.**

These are the words you may be able to identify as positive or negative. By the way, we don't mean to suggest that you should try this technique with words you've never encountered before. Looking at a mystery word and saying, "Hmm, I don't like the look of that word," doesn't count. You have to have seen it before and have a vague sense of what it means.

You may not know the exact meaning of each of the words above (remember to look them up when you're done with this example—several are from the Hit Parade), but you may have a *feeling* about whether each is positive or negative.

As it turns out, "censured," "rebuked," "rebutted," and "undermined" are all negative words. Because you are looking for a generally positive word to fill the blank, you can eliminate all four of them—or as many of them as you have a negative feeling about. The correct answer is "lauded," which means "praised."

TWO-BLANK SENTENCE COMPLETION

About half of the sentence completions on the SAT contain two blanks instead of one. The same clues we've already discussed above are vital in answering these questions, but to use these clues effectively, it helps to concentrate on one blank at a time. Think about it this way: When you go to buy a new pair of shoes, you can eliminate pairs that don't fit after trying on just one. If the left shoe doesn't fit, you don't bother trying on the right shoe. So try one blank at a time. If the answer choice doesn't fit for that one blank, you can eliminate it. Which blank should you start with? Whichever you think is easiest. Try the following sentence:

5. Although the food at the restaurant was usually -------, the main course was ------- by an overabundance of salt.

    (A) bland . . enhanced
    (B) indifferent . . supplanted
    (C) delectable . . marred
    (D) distinguished . . elevated
    (E) diverse . . superb

THE PRINCETON REVIEW METHOD

Step One   Cover the answer choices and read the entire sentence. Decide which blank you think would be easier for you to fill in with your own word. In this case, the first clause of the sentence, which contains the first blank ("Although the food at the restaurant was usually -------"), is not very helpful. The food might be delicious, or it might be terrible. You just don't know yet. Concentrate instead on the second clause of the sentence: "The main course was ------- by an overabundance of salt." How would you describe food to which much too much salt has been added? If you chose words like "ruined" or "spoiled" or "flawed," you were right on track.

In two-blank sentence completions, attack the blanks one at a time.

Step Two	Completely ignoring the first word in each answer choice, take a look at the *second* word in each answer choice. You are looking for a word like "ruined." Clearly, choices A, "enhanced," D, "elevated," and E, "superb," are all wrong. Physically cross them off. Before you've even looked at the first blank, you're down to two possible choices!
Step Three	Look at the first blank to decide between the two remaining choices. You've figured out that the second half of the sentence is saying that the food was bad. Did you notice that the first half of the sentence began with a trigger word? The word "although" told you that the second half of the sentence would contradict the first half. Let's summarize what you know about the sentence so far:

> Although the food at the restaurant was
> usually -------, tonight it was (something
> negative).

What kind of word are you looking for in the first blank? If you suggested "delicious" or "good" or "tasty," you were right on track. Look at the answer choices.

(A) **already eliminated**
(B) indifferent . . supplanted
(C) delectable . . marred
(D) **already eliminated**
(E) **already eliminated**

Remember that you have already crossed off three choices just by looking at the second blank. You're down to two remaining choices. Looking only at the first word in each, which do you think is closest to "delicious"? If you said choice C, you are 10 points ahead. "Delectable" means "highly pleasing." "Marred" (meaning "flawed") was much better than "supplanted" (meaning "to take the place of").

TWO-BLANK POSITIVE/NEGATIVE

On two-blank problems, you will sometimes need to watch out for the relationship between the two blanks. For instance, the blanks will often have a generally positive/generally negative relationship. Take a look at the question below:

> Although he was ------- by nature, his duties as
> a prison guard forced him to be more -------.

As always, try to supply your own words before you look at the answer choices, but sometimes (as in this case) the sentence is a little too vague to supply precise words. Work with what you have. Did you notice the trigger word "although" at the beginning of the sentence? Because of this, you know that the first half of the sentence will contradict the second half. What kind of clues do you have in this sentence? In the second phrase, the sentence discusses how he must behave as a prison guard.

If you had to guess, do you think the second blank is going to be a generally positive word or a generally negative word? Even though you don't know exactly what the word will be, the second blank is likely to be negative. And *that* means that the first blank is likely to be positive.

Now look at the answer choices. It sometimes helps to actually write into the blanks the directions you think the words will go in, as shown:

6. Although he was (<u>positive word</u>) by nature,
   his duties as a prison guard forced him to be
   more (<u>negative word</u>).

   (A) hermetic . . lonely
   (B) lenient . . strict
   (C) unhappy . . stylized
   (D) gentle . . witty
   (E) trite . . tactful

Even though you have a general idea of both blanks, it still makes sense to work on one at a time. You are looking for a generally negative word for the second blank. So eliminate any choices whose second words are positive. That gets rid of choices D, "witty," and E, "tactful." Cross them off with your pencil. Now look at the first blank in the answer choices that remain. The first blank should be generally positive, which means you can get rid of choices A, "hermetic," and C, "unhappy," as well. There's only one answer left: It must be choice B. Read the sentence again with "lenient" and "strict," just to make sure. Does one word contradict the other? Yes. Does the sentence make sense? You bet!

NEGATIVE/POSITIVE? POSITIVE/NEGATIVE? WHO KNOWS?

The most difficult sentence completions are probably the ones in which all you know is the relationship between the blanks. Take a look at the following, and note the trigger word:

> Although he was ------- by nature, he has
> recently become more -------.

All that you really know about the missing two words in this sentence is that they must be opposites. Fortunately, problems like this appear infrequently on the SAT. When they do show up, you will be forced to go to the answer choices in search of opposites.

(A) generous . . frugal
(B) liberal . . dependable
(C) insensitive . . indifferent
(D) practical . . cooperative
(E) knowledgeable . . casual

Which pair of words above are opposites? The correct answer is choice A.

QUICK QUIZ #4

In each of the following sentences, try to decide whether the blanks should be positive or negative, or whether it is impossible to tell.

1. The new law will be very unpopular with the citizens of New Mexico because it ------- many ------- beliefs.

2. Despite the ------- of the men and women in the rescue team, their effort was -------.

3. The team had looked forward to the semifinal match with great -------, but the event proved to be -------.

4. Unlike their ------- ancestors, the whales of today are -------.

5. For all their apparent -------, the rich are just as ------- as the poor when it comes to an earthquake.

ANSWERS AND EXPLANATIONS: QUICK QUIZ #4

1. – then +. The two words were "debunks" and "popular."

2. + then –. The two words were "courage" and "useless."

3. + then –. The two words were "enthusiasm" and "a debacle."

4. + then – or – then +. While you can't tell exactly what the values of the blanks are, you know they must be opposites. The two words were "solitary" and "gregarious."

5. + then –. The two words were "advantages" and "vulnerable."

GUESSING AND PACING

Even if you don't know some of the vocabulary words in a sentence completion, it is difficult to imagine a case in which you won't be able to eliminate at least one answer choice using the techniques we've just shown you. And if you eliminate one answer choice or more, then you *must* guess on the problem.

How long should you spend on each group of sentence completions? About four to six minutes, if you plan to finish the Critical Reading section. This works out to 40–45 seconds per problem. Of course, in the real world, you won't spend exactly the same amount of time on each question; some will take 10 seconds, others will take much longer. Use the practice sections that follow to work on your pacing.

SENTENCE COMPLETION CHECKLIST

1. As you read the sentences, cover up the answer choices and look for

   • The clue (meaning from the context of the sentence)

   • Trigger words (------- and -------: two words are usually similar; ------- but ------- : two words are usually opposed)

   • Degree of difficulty clues (easy questions have easy answers; hard questions have hard answers)

2. When there are two blanks, do them one at a time.

3. If you're having trouble with the meaning of the sentence or the individual words in the answer choices, think + or −.

4. Remember that it's often easier to eliminate wrong answer choices than to pick the right choice.

SENTENCE COMPLETIONS: PROBLEM SET 1

Directions: For each question in this section, select the best answer from among the choices given and fill in the corresponding oval on the answer sheet.

Each sentence below has one or two blanks, each blank indicating that something has been omitted. Beneath the sentence are five words or sets of words labeled A through E. Choose the word or set of words that, when inserted in the sentence, <u>best</u> fits the meaning of the sentence as a whole.

Example:

Medieval kingdoms did not become constitutional republics overnight; on the contrary, the change was -------.

(A) unpopular   (B) unexpected   (C) advantageous
(D) sufficient   (E) gradual

Ⓐ Ⓑ Ⓒ Ⓓ ●

Recommended time: 4 to 5 minutes

1. The shark possesses ------- sense of smell; in experiments, a small quantity of blood released into the ocean has ------- sharks from as far away as three quarters of a mile.

    (A) a cautious . . maimed
    (B) a keen . . attracted
    (C) a deficient . . enticed
    (D) a negligent . . repelled
    (E) a foul . . frightened

2. When the computer chip first became available, many companies were quick to ------- it, hoping to ------- this technological innovation.

    (A) reject . . benefit from
    (B) deflate . . succeed with
    (C) deny . . participate in
    (D) embrace . . profit from
    (E) accept . . escape from

3. The witness accused the young man of breaking the window, but later ------- the accusation.

    (A) recanted
    (B) recounted
    (C) predicted
    (D) arranged
    (E) supported

4. In his extraordinary ------- of the daily life of the early colonists, the historian captured the ------- hardships of the first winter.

    (A) revelation . . tranquil
    (B) evocation . . bleak
    (C) premonition . . dreary
    (D) exacerbation . . tacit
    (E) celebration . . blithe

5. Character traits that are quickly learned in social settings can often be altered just as quickly; by contrast, ------- characteristics are more difficult to -------.

    (A) credible . . respect
    (B) trivial . . protect
    (C) abrupt . . supply
    (D) tasteless . . believe
    (E) innate . . modify

6. Although the number of opening moves in the game of chess is not -------, there are more than enough to confuse the beginner.

    (A) circumscribed
    (B) measurable
    (C) estimable
    (D) familiar
    (E) infinite

7. The Big Bang theory is regarded as the most likely explanation for the beginning of the universe, but a few scientists, who regard the theory as -------, continue to search for an -------.

(A) practical . . estimate
(B) proven . . objective
(C) implausible . . alternative
(D) controversial . . agenda
(E) comprehensive . . answer

8. The composer saw his latest composition not as ------- the music he had traditionally composed but rather as a ------- progression.

(A) a continuation of . . lurid
(B) an alternative to . . contradictory
(C) an affront to . . despotic
(D) a departure from . . logical
(E) an interpretation of . . reasonable

1 ⊂A⊃ ⊂B⊃ ⊂C⊃ ⊂D⊃ ⊂E⊃
2 ⊂A⊃ ⊂B⊃ ⊂C⊃ ⊂D⊃ ⊂E⊃
3 ⊂A⊃ ⊂B⊃ ⊂C⊃ ⊂D⊃ ⊂E⊃
4 ⊂A⊃ ⊂B⊃ ⊂C⊃ ⊂D⊃ ⊂E⊃
5 ⊂A⊃ ⊂B⊃ ⊂C⊃ ⊂D⊃ ⊂E⊃
6 ⊂A⊃ ⊂B⊃ ⊂C⊃ ⊂D⊃ ⊂E⊃
7 ⊂A⊃ ⊂B⊃ ⊂C⊃ ⊂D⊃ ⊂E⊃
8 ⊂A⊃ ⊂B⊃ ⊂C⊃ ⊂D⊃ ⊂E⊃

WORDS YOU DIDN'T KNOW FROM PROBLEM SET 1

Before you check your answers below, take a minute to write down the words you didn't know from the previous questions. Look them up and review them tomorrow.

Word	Definition
_____	_____
_____	_____
_____	_____
_____	_____
_____	_____

ANSWERS AND EXPLANATIONS: PROBLEM SET 1

There are 8 sentence completions in this section, so you know that the first two or three will be relatively easy, the second three or four will be medium, and the last two or three will be relatively difficult. Did you remember not to skip any questions?

1. **B** Attack the first blank first. If the shark has no sense of smell to speak of, then it would be neither attracted to nor repelled by the blood in the water; the shark simply wouldn't know the blood was there. Thus, you want a word that indicates the shark has a "good" sense of smell. Looking at the answer choices, you can eliminate choices C, "a deficient," and D, "a negligent." Can anyone have a "cautious" sense of smell? Not really. And just to check, even if the shark did have a cautious sense of smell, how would the smell of blood "maim" the shark? Eliminate choice A. A "foul" smell is an expression you have probably heard, but a foul sense of smell? Not too likely. To check, would a shark be frightened by the smell of blood? Not the sharks we knew and loved in *Jaws I* and *II*. Eliminate choice E. If the shark's sense of smell were "keen," then it would be attracted to the blood. The correct answer is choice B.

2. **D** This is one of the infrequent sentence completions in which the sentence itself does not completely clue you in as to which words will best answer the question. For example, the sentence could use two positive words to read,

...many

companies were quick to utilize it, hoping to succeed with this technological innovation. Or it could use two negative words to read,

...many

companies were quick to dismiss it, hoping to ignore this technological innovation.

Either of these would be fine. So what you have to do here is look at the answer choices for either two positive words or two negative words. Choice A is – then + , choice B is – then + , choice C is – then + , choice D is + then + , and choice E is + then –. The correct answer is choice D.

3. **A** The trigger word ("but") signifies that the witness does something in the second half of the sentence that is somewhat contradictory to what he or she does in the first half of the sentence—and the only thing the witness does in the first half is to accuse the young man. What would be contradictory to making an accusation? The correct answer is choice A.

4. **B** In this question, the second blank is probably easier to start with. "Hardships" is a negative sort of word, so you can expect that the adjective used to describe it will be negative as well. This allows you to eliminate choices A, "tranquil," D, "tacit" (meaning "implied, or not stated outright"), and E, "blithe" (meaning "joyous").

Choices B and C remain, so look now at the first blank.

Choice C, "premonition" (meaning "a feeling that something is about to happen"), is unlikely. How could a historian have a premonition about something that happened 200 years ago? The correct answer is choice B. An "evocation" means "a bringing forth."

5. **E** The trigger words ("by contrast") signify that the first blank describes character traits that contradict the "quickly learned" character traits described at the beginning of the sentence. Which of the first words in the answer choices is a rough opposite of "quickly learned"? Choice E, "innate" (meaning "existing in a person since birth"), is the only one.

Suppose for a minute that you aren't sure of the meaning of "innate." You would now have to tackle the second blank. The first half of the sentence talks about traits that "can be altered...quickly." The second half, by contrast, talks about traits "that are harder to -------." What word do you think might fit in this blank? If you said "change" or "altered," you are right on the money. The correct answer is choice E.

6. **E**   Here's a summary of this sentence using the trigger word:

> Although -------, there's more than enough.

If we were talking about money, we might say, "Although we don't have all the money in the world, there's more than enough for us." If we were talking about a Thanksgiving turkey, we might say, "It isn't the biggest turkey in the world, but it's more than enough for us."

If we are talking about the number of opening chess moves, we would say, "The number of moves isn't infinite, but it's more than enough to confuse us."

7. **C**   The trigger word ("but") signifies that the "few scientists" don't completely agree with the Big Bang theory. Tackle the first blank. Which of the answer choices implies doubt about the theory? Both choices C and D imply doubt. Thus, eliminate choices A, B, and E. If you don't buy one theory, do you search for an alternative or an agenda? The correct answer is choice C.

8. **D**   The trigger word here is "not as [one thing] but rather as [something else]." Thus, the second half of the sentence is likely to contradict the first half.

If you check the answer choices for the different possible first words, you will notice that they are all nouns: "a continuation," "an alternative." The construction "not as [one thing] but rather as [something else]" must always compare two nouns. The possible second words are all adjectives describing the noun "progression."

This means the first blank must be a noun that contradicts the noun "progression." Rule out choice A, "a continuation," because it is almost a synonym. Choices C and E have nothing to do with contradicting a progression, so eliminate them as well.

Choices B and D contradict the notion of a progression, so hold onto them.

Now look at the second blank in the two remaining choices. The second blank is an adjective describing "progression." Which makes more sense? A "logical" progression or a "contradictory" progression? The best answer is choice D.

SENTENCE COMPLETIONS: PROBLEM SET 2

Directions: For each question in this section, select the best answer from among the choices given and fill in the corresponding oval on the answer sheet.

Each sentence below has one or two blanks, each blank indicating that something has been omitted. Beneath the sentence are five words or sets of words labeled A through E. Choose the word or set of words that, when inserted in the sentence, <u>best</u> fits the meaning of the sentence as a whole.

Example:

Medieval kingdoms did not become constitutional republics overnight; on the contrary, the change was -------.

(A) unpopular   (B) unexpected   (C) advantageous
(D) sufficient   (E) gradual

Ⓐ Ⓑ Ⓒ Ⓓ ●

Recommended time: 3 to 4 minutes

1. Though he claimed that the computer he had just purchased contained the latest features, in fact it was already -------.

    (A) expensive
    (B) obsolete
    (C) technical
    (D) unreliable
    (E) impressive

2. For most film audiences, the ------- of a scary event is more ------- than the event itself.

    (A) anticipation . . frightening
    (B) expectation . . skeptical
    (C) experience . . mundane
    (D) application . . interesting
    (E) unfolding . . formal

3. Although Laura's uncle was ------- by nature, he was always ------- for his luncheon dates with his niece.

    (A) predictable . . on time
    (B) tardy . . punctual
    (C) generous . . late
    (D) unstable . . tardy
    (E) hostile . . unprepared

4. In their efforts to ------- the existence of a new strain of bacteria, scientists may be ------- by the lack of a suitable microscope.

    (A) establish . . hampered
    (B) eradicate . . aided
    (C) disprove . . defined
    (D) justify . . hindered
    (E) substantiate . . unmoved

5. The doctor not only had ------- for the new treatment, but he also found it -------.

    (A) a contempt . . necessary
    (B) an esteem . . contagious
    (C) a fondness . . irredeemable
    (D) a disgust . . repugnant
    (E) a weakness . . irrational

1 ⊂A⊃ ⊂B⊃ ⊂C⊃ ⊂D⊃ ⊂E⊃
2 ⊂A⊃ ⊂B⊃ ⊂C⊃ ⊂D⊃ ⊂E⊃
3 ⊂A⊃ ⊂B⊃ ⊂C⊃ ⊂D⊃ ⊂E⊃
4 ⊂A⊃ ⊂B⊃ ⊂C⊃ ⊂D⊃ ⊂E⊃
5 ⊂A⊃ ⊂B⊃ ⊂C⊃ ⊂D⊃ ⊂E⊃

WORDS YOU DIDN'T KNOW FROM PROBLEM SET 2

Before you check your answers below, take a minute to write down the words you didn't know from the previous questions. Look them up and review them tomorrow.

Word	Definition
_____	_____
_____	_____
_____	_____
_____	_____
_____	_____
_____	_____

ANSWERS AND EXPLANATIONS: PROBLEM SET 2

There are 5 sentence completions in this section, so you know that the first one or two will be relatively easy, the middle one will be medium, and the last one or two will be relatively difficult. Did you remember not to skip any questions?

1. **B** While most of the adjectives in the answer choices could describe a computer, the structure of the sentence provides a clue. The clue in this sentence is the phrase "the latest features." However, the trigger word that begins the sentence ("though") tells you that the second half of the sentence is in opposition to the first. What would be the opposite of something that has all the latest features? That's right: obsolete.

2. **A** The construction "...of a scary event is more ------- than the event itself," makes it likely that the second blank will just be another word for "scary."

3. **B** The trigger word ("although") signifies that the second word is going to be in opposition to the first word. In choices A and D, the two pairs of words are not in opposition to each other—rather the reverse. In choices C and E the two pairs of words are unrelated to each other. Only choice B provides opposites: a "tardy" person is unlikely to be "punctual."

4. **A** The best clues in this sentence are the three words "the lack of." It seems like "the lack of" a suitable microscope would be a problem for a scientist. Thus, the second blank needs to be filled by a word like "hampered" or "hindered." To fill in the first blank, consider what a bunch of scientists would want to do about the existence of a new strain of bacteria. Well, they might want to eradicate (or destroy) the bacteria, but they wouldn't want to eradicate the existence of the bacteria. Also, scientists wouldn't be "aided" by the lack of a microscope. They might want to do things like "disprove" or "substantiate" but they wouldn't be "defined" or "unmoved" by the lack of a microscope.

5. **D** Unlike a simple trigger word, the construction "not only...but also..." implies two thoughts that are quite similar. Thus you are looking for either two positive words or two negative words.

This is a difficult question (number 5 out of 5) so be on the lookout for Joe Bloggs answers. Choice B, containing the word "contagious," might be very tempting to Joe because the stem sentence is about a doctor. Eliminate it simply because Joe wants to pick it. Each of the other answer choices mixes a negative word with a positive word except for choice D.

SENTENCE COMPLETION: PROBLEM SET 3

Directions: For each question in this section, select the best answer from among the choices given and fill in the corresponding oval on the answer sheet.

Each sentence below has one or two blanks, each blank indicating that something has been omitted. Beneath the sentence are five words or sets of words labeled A through E. Choose the word or set of words that, when inserted in the sentence, <u>best</u> fits the meaning of the sentence as a whole.

Example:

Medieval kingdoms did not become constitutional republics overnight; on the contrary, the change was -------.

(A) unpopular   (B) unexpected   (C) advantageous
(D) sufficient   (E) gradual

Ⓐ Ⓑ Ⓒ Ⓓ ●

Recommended time: 3 to 4 minutes

1. The city planner argued that the proposed convention center would create new traffic patterns, some of them benign, but others potentially -------.

   (A) unexpected
   (B) productive
   (C) older
   (D) harmful
   (E) conventional

2. It is unclear whether the new treatment will be approved for general use because its ------- has not yet been -------.

   (A) usefulness . . denied
   (B) diversity . . proven
   (C) effectiveness . . established
   (D) performance . . preserved
   (E) integrity . . lampooned

3. Henrietta behaves in such ------- manner that no one expects her to accomplish anything.

   (A) an intelligent
   (B) a zealous
   (C) a slothful
   (D) an imperious
   (E) an efficient

4. The young children, who willingly stood in line for hours to get the basketball star's autograph, referred to him only in the most ------- terms.

   (A) cynical
   (B) detrimental
   (C) neutral
   (D) objective
   (E) reverential

5. When choosing works of art, museum curators should base their selections not on the artists' current ------- but rather on the artists' ------- qualities, for the public can be very fickle.

   (A) tableaus . . trivial
   (B) standing . . capricious
   (C) renown . . enduring
   (D) aesthetics . . impudent
   (E) philanthropy . . innocuous

6. In her later paintings, the artist exchanged her wild brush strokes and chaotic layerings of paint for ------- attention to detail that verged on fussiness.

   (A) a bohemian
   (B) a fastidious
   (C) an unconventional
   (D) an indelible
   (E) an opaque

1 ⊂A⊃ ⊂B⊃ ⊂C⊃ ⊂D⊃ ⊂E⊃
2 ⊂A⊃ ⊂B⊃ ⊂C⊃ ⊂D⊃ ⊂E⊃
3 ⊂A⊃ ⊂B⊃ ⊂C⊃ ⊂D⊃ ⊂E⊃
4 ⊂A⊃ ⊂B⊃ ⊂C⊃ ⊂D⊃ ⊂E⊃
5 ⊂A⊃ ⊂B⊃ ⊂C⊃ ⊂D⊃ ⊂E⊃
6 ⊂A⊃ ⊂B⊃ ⊂C⊃ ⊂D⊃ ⊂E⊃

WORDS YOU DIDN'T KNOW FROM PROBLEM SET 3

Before you check your answers below, take a minute to write down the words you didn't know from the previous questions. Look them up and review them tomorrow.

Word   **Definition**

_____   _____

_____   _____

_____   _____

_____   _____

_____   _____

ANSWERS AND EXPLANATIONS: PROBLEM SET 3

There are six sentence completions in this section, so you know that the first two will be relatively easy, the second two will be medium, and the last two will be relatively difficult. Did you remember not to skip any questions?

1. **D** Again, the trigger word ("but") signifies that you are looking for a word that is in opposition to something that comes before—but which something? If you picked choice C, you thought the missing word should oppose the "new" traffic patterns. However, in this sentence, the clue is the word "benign" and the "but" is contrasting two types of traffic patterns: "some of them benign...but others -------." Thus, you need a word that means the opposite of "benign."

2. **C** In order for the treatment to be approved, it will have to be shown to be effective. Therefore, the first blank has to be a positive word such as "effectiveness," and the second word should also be a positive word, such as "proven." In choice A, "usefulness" is positive, but "denied" is negative. In choice B, "diversity" is positive but it doesn't seem like a word that describes a positive attribute for a treatment. Choice C gives you two positive words. In choice D, "performance" might be okay, but would "preserving" a treatment help to get it approved? Choice E also gives you a positive first word, but the second word, "lampooned," is negative.

3. **C** Because no one expects Henrietta to accomplish anything, you have to assume that she is putting out some kind of negative attitude. Which answer choices are negative? Both choices C and D are possibilities. If she "imperious," Henrietta would arrogantly order people around, and she might actually get a lot done, so eliminate choice D. "Slothful" means lazy and sluggish.

4. **E** If the children willingly stood in line for hours to get the star's autograph, that implies that they think well of him. Thus, look for a positive word to fill in the blank. "Objective" might be considered a positive word, but it doesn't have the connotation of respect that the children seemed to be showing. The best answer is choice E.

5. **C** In this tough question, the trigger word ("but") is helpful, but only up to a point, because the vocabulary is difficult. The second blank is probably the best place to start. What kinds of qualities do you think ETS would want museum curators to look for in an artist? If you said "good" qualities, you were exactly right. Looking at the second words in the answer choices, can you eliminate any because they were not good? Yes, if you know what they mean. Choice A, "trivial," choice B, "capricious" (meaning "impulsive, whimsical") and choice D, "impudent" (meaning "disrespectful or rude"), can all be crossed off. Choice C, "enduring," is good, so hold onto that. Choice E, "innocuous" (meaning "causing or intending little harm"), is mildly good, so do not eliminate it either.

Now look at the first words in the two remaining choices. The word "renown" means "fame." The word "philanthropy" means "the practice of giving money or support to worthy causes." A philanthropic artist might be of help to a museum, but this sentence suggests the curator ignores philanthropy in favor of an artist who causes little harm. That doesn't sound right. The correct answer is choice C.

6. **B** The clues here are that the artist "exchanged" wild and chaotic stuff for something else, presumably quite different. What would be an adjective very different from "wild" and "chaotic" that would describe "...attention to detail that verged on fussiness"? If you are thinking words like "conservative" or "careful" you are right on track.

Look at the answer choices. "Bohemian" (meaning "setting social conventions aside") is clearly wrong, as is "unconventional." "Fastidious" (meaning "careful with details") seems pretty good. "Indelible" (meaning "incapable of being erased") and "opaque" (meaning "not transparent") are both artsy words and so might seem tempting in this sentence about an artist, but neither means "careful." The correct answer is choice B.

SENTENCE COMPLETION: PROBLEM SET 4

Directions: For each question in this section, select the best answer from among the choices given and fill in the corresponding oval on the answer sheet.

Each sentence below has one or two blanks, each blank indicating that something has been omitted. Beneath the sentence are five words or sets of words labeled A through E. Choose the word or set of words that, when inserted in the sentence, <u>best</u> fits the meaning of the sentence as a whole.

Example:

Medieval kingdoms did not become constitutional republics overnight; on the contrary, the change was -------.

(A) unpopular   (B) unexpected   (C) advantageous
(D) sufficient   (E) gradual

Ⓐ Ⓑ Ⓒ Ⓓ ●

Recommended time: 3 to 4 minutes

1. The orator was so ------- that even those who were not interested in the subject matter found themselves staying awake.

   (A) tactful
   (B) listless
   (C) pious
   (D) intriguing
   (E) sullen

2. To make sure their ------- would be heard, the coal workers went on strike to protest the ------- lack of safety precautions in the mines.

   (A) voices . . generous
   (B) demands . . deplorable
   (C) complaints . . uneventful
   (D) neighbors . . dangerous
   (E) case . . immaculate

3. In his review, Greenburg argues that the ------- nature of this artist's paintings ------- the artist's conviction that the twentieth century has spun wildly out of control.

   (A) chaotic . . reflects
   (B) controlled . . demonstrates
   (C) disordered . . belies
   (D) symmetrical . . interprets
   (E) dangerous . . saps

4. A recent barrage of media reports on the health benefits of physical activity has fostered a national ------- exercise, but new studies show surprisingly little ------- in the life expectancy of people who exercise.

   (A) preoccupation with . . improvement
   (B) revulsion toward . . increase
   (C) obsession with . . decline
   (D) conception of . . speculation
   (E) solution to . . reduction

5. Previous to the discovery of one intact ancient burial site in Central America, it had been thought that all of the Mayan tombs had been ------- by thieves.

   (A) eradicated
   (B) exacerbated
   (C) prevaricated
   (D) subordinated
   (E) desecrated

1 ⊂A⊃ ⊂B⊃ ⊂C⊃ ⊂D⊃ ⊂E⊃
2 ⊂A⊃ ⊂B⊃ ⊂C⊃ ⊂D⊃ ⊂E⊃
3 ⊂A⊃ ⊂B⊃ ⊂C⊃ ⊂D⊃ ⊂E⊃
4 ⊂A⊃ ⊂B⊃ ⊂C⊃ ⊂D⊃ ⊂E⊃
5 ⊂A⊃ ⊂B⊃ ⊂C⊃ ⊂D⊃ ⊂E⊃

WORDS YOU DIDN'T KNOW FROM PROBLEM SET 4

Before you check your answers below, take a minute to write down the words you didn't know from the previous questions. Look them up and review them tomorrow.

Word

_____

_____

_____

_____

_____

Definition

_____

_____

_____

_____

_____

ANSWERS AND EXPLANATIONS: PROBLEM SET 4

There are 5 sentence completions in this section, so you know that the first one or two will be relatively easy, the middle one will be medium, and the last one or two will be relatively difficult. Did you remember not to skip any questions?

1. **D** What kind of speaker would make people stay awake even when they were not interested in what he was talking about? An *intriguing* speaker.

2. **B** Most people might choose to tackle the first blank first, and they would probably guess that the first word would be something like "demands." Unfortunately, a quick look at the answer choices shows you that four of the five alternatives sound possible. Oh well. Try the second blank. Do you think the lack of safety precautions in a coal mine would be a good thing or a bad thing? Obviously, the adjective describing this lack is going to be a negative word. So eliminate everything but choices B and D. Looking now at the first word in the two choices that remain, it is easy to see that "neighbors" makes no real sense.

3. **A** It seems likely that the artist's conviction (that things are out of control) might have something to do with the art he or she produces. Choice A works on this level. Choice B does not, for a "controlled" painting style doesn't demonstrate a world gone out of control. Choice C doesn't either, for a "disordered" style would not "belie" (meaning "expose as false") a world gone out of control. In choice D, a "symmetrical" style would not "interpret" a world gone out of control. Why would a painter's style of painting "sap" (meaning "to drain away") his or her convictions? The best answer is choice A.

4. **A** The trigger word "but" signifies that the second part of the sentence is likely to somehow contradict the supposed health benefits of exercise. Attack the second blank first: ". . . new studies show surprisingly little ------- in the life expectancy of people who exercise." Considering that the result is surprising, what do you think the word should be? If you said "rise" or "increase" you were right on target.

Look at the answer choices. Choices C and E can be ruled out right away, because they are headed in the opposite direction. Choice D doesn't make a lot of sense.

Now look at the first words in the two remaining answer choices. Choice A, "preoccupation with," seems right. Choice B, "revulsion toward," might be all right if the structural clue "but" had not been there. The correct answer is choice A.

5. **E** It's pretty clear from the context that you are looking for a word like "destroyed" here. Unfortunately, because this was the fifth question out of five, the vocabulary is very tough. Even the positive/negative technique is not helpful here, because *all* the words are negative. The only real way to get this is to know the meaning of the correct word. "Desecrate" means "to abuse something sacred." "Exacerbate" means "to make something worse." "Prevaricate" means "to lie." "Subordinate" means "to place in a lower order." "Eradicate" means "to root out," which might have seemed tempting, but didn't give the sense of destruction of something sacred. The best answer is choice E.

SENTENCE COMPLETION: PROBLEM SET 5

Directions: For each question in this section, select the best answer from among the choices given and fill in the corresponding oval on the answer sheet.

Each sentence below has one or two blanks, each blank indicating that something has been omitted. Beneath the sentence are five words or sets of words labeled A through E. Choose the word or set of words that, when inserted in the sentence, <u>best</u> fits the meaning of the sentence as a whole.

Example:

Medieval kingdoms did not become constitutional republics overnight; on the contrary, the change was -------.

(A) unpopular   (B) unexpected   (C) advantageous
(D) sufficient   (E) gradual

Ⓐ Ⓑ Ⓒ Ⓓ ●

Recommended time: 5 to 6 minutes

1. The association agreed to ------- one of its members when she was discovered to have ------- an infraction of the association rules.

   (A) discipline . . prevented
   (B) denounce . . impeded
   (C) censure . . committed
   (D) honor . . supported
   (E) promote . . aided

2. While old books are often considered ------- by modern readers, librarians see them as historic documents that allow us to look back through time.

   (A) reclusive
   (B) fascinating
   (C) detrimental
   (D) relevant
   (E) obsolete

3. The robin, a bird common to the Northeast, is neither rare nor reclusive, but is as ------- and ------- a bird as you can find.

   (A) wily . . tolerant
   (B) amicable . . wary
   (C) commonplace . . amiable
   (D) vulnerable . . capable
   (E) powerful . . fragile

4. The professor's lecturing style was certainly -------, but he told his students that in teaching such a complicated subject, clarity was more important than levity.

   (A) scintillating
   (B) unbiased
   (C) monotonous
   (D) arrogant
   (E) stimulating

5. During a ten-year period, Napoleon conquered most of the Baltic States and ------- Spain as well.

   (A) vanquished
   (B) forfeited
   (C) reiterated
   (D) transcended
   (E) refuted

6. Unlike the unequivocal accounts provided by eyewitnesses, the evidence provided by the flight recorder was more -------, leading to the development of several different theories to explain the crash.

   (A) indisputable
   (B) ambiguous
   (C) lucid
   (D) infallible
   (E) theoretical

7. Engineers attribute the building's ------- during the earthquake, which destroyed more rigid structures, to the surprising ------- of its steel girders.

(A) obliteration . . strength
(B) damage . . weakness
(C) survival . . inadequacy
(D) endurance . . suppleness
(E) devastation . . inflexibility

8. By nature he was -------, generally limiting his comments to ------- remarks.

(A) reticent . . terse
(B) stoic . . superfluous
(C) trite . . concise
(D) verbose . . succinct
(E) arrogant . . self-effacing

1 ⊂A⊃ ⊂B⊃ ⊂C⊃ ⊂D⊃ ⊂E⊃
2 ⊂A⊃ ⊂B⊃ ⊂C⊃ ⊂D⊃ ⊂E⊃
3 ⊂A⊃ ⊂B⊃ ⊂C⊃ ⊂D⊃ ⊂E⊃
4 ⊂A⊃ ⊂B⊃ ⊂C⊃ ⊂D⊃ ⊂E⊃
5 ⊂A⊃ ⊂B⊃ ⊂C⊃ ⊂D⊃ ⊂E⊃
6 ⊂A⊃ ⊂B⊃ ⊂C⊃ ⊂D⊃ ⊂E⊃
7 ⊂A⊃ ⊂B⊃ ⊂C⊃ ⊂D⊃ ⊂E⊃
8 ⊂A⊃ ⊂B⊃ ⊂C⊃ ⊂D⊃ ⊂E⊃

WORDS YOU DIDN'T KNOW FROM PROBLEM SET 5

Before you check your answers below, take a minute to write down the words you didn't know from the previous questions. Look them up and review them tomorrow.

Word	Definition
_____	_____
_____	_____
_____	_____
_____	_____
_____	_____
_____	_____

ANSWERS AND EXPLANATIONS: PROBLEM SET 5

There are 8 sentence completions in this section, so you know that the first two or three will be relatively easy, the second three or four will be medium, and the last two or three will be relatively difficult. Did you remember not to skip any questions?

1. **C** If the association member took part in the infraction, then it seems almost certain that the association will punish her. While it was just possible that the sentence was going to go the other way—i.e., they were going to reward her for discovering the infraction—the first possibility was more likely. Look through the answer choices and pick the one that works. The answer is choice C.

2. **E** The trigger word "while" opposes librarians' views of old books and those of modern readers. How do you think librarians are likely to feel about old books? If you said "positive," you are right on track. That means the modern readers will feel negative. This gets us down to choices A, C, or E. Choice E is the best answer.

3. **C** When ETS sets up pairs of words in opposition (trigger word: "but") as it does here, it helps to deal with the pairs in the correct order: The robin is not "rare" but -------; not "reclusive" but -------. Thus, for the first blank you want a word that means "not rare." For the second blank you want a word that means "not reclusive." The correct answer is choice C.

4. **C** The second half of the sentence following the trigger word "but" tells you that the professor is clearer than he is funny. So his style is "not funny." Which of the answer choices is closest to "not funny"? That's right, the answer is choice C.

5. **A** The trigger word "and" signifies that the two verbs of the sentence are going to be similar. Napoleon conquered the Baltic states and conquered Spain as well. So you need a word like "conquered." The correct answer is choice A.

6. **B** The trigger word "unlike" signifies that the recorder's evidence is the opposite of "unequivocal." If you know what "unequivocal" means, this is a great clue. But if you don't, there is another clue later in the sentence: The evidence of the flight recorder led to several different theories. What kind of evidence would lead to several different theories? "Indisputable" evidence? Not likely. "Ambiguous" evidence? That sounds correct! "Lucid" (meaning "clear") evidence? No. "Infallible" (meaning "unable to be proven wrong") evidence? No. "Theoretical" evidence? Maybe, but "ambiguous" is better. The correct answer is choice B. "Unequivocal" means "certain, not open to interpretation."

7. **D** The clue here is the phrase ". . .which destroyed more rigid structures." Obviously, unlike other buildings that were more rigid, this building didn't fall down. Attack the first blank first. What word would you pick to describe this building's performance during the earthquake? If you were thinking of words like "survival" or "strength," then you were right on track.

Eliminate any answers that suggest the building was destroyed: choices A, B, and E. You are left with choices C and D. Now look at the second blank. Do you think the building's survival hinged on the "inadequacy" of its girders or the "suppleness" (meaning "the ability to bend easily") of its girders? "Inadequacy" is certainly wrong, but at first, you might think "suppleness" sounded wrong too. The two contextual clues here were "...more rigid structures," and ". . .the surprising _____." Steel girders are not usually thought of as being "supple," which is why the word "surprising" is appropriate.

8. **A** What makes this a difficult question is its lack of clues. Really, there is only one small clue: the word "limiting." And one small trigger word: The second half of the sentence is not going to contradict the first half—it is going to continue in the same direction. With these two clues noted, take a look at the answer choices.

If he were "reticent" (meaning "untalkative, shy"), would this person limit himself to "terse" (meaning "brief, free of extra words") remarks? Sure. Just check the other answer choices. If he were "stoic" (meaning "having great emotional control"), would he limit himself to "superfluous" (meaning "unnecessary") remarks? No. If he were "trite" (meaning "overused, lacking freshness"), would he limit himself to "concise" remarks? No. If he were "verbose" (meaning "talkative"), would he limit himself to "succinct" (meaning "concise") remarks? No. If he were "arrogant" (meaning "overconfident"), would he limit himself to "self-effacing" (meaning "putting yourself last") remarks? No way! The answer is choice A.

SENTENCE COMPLETION: PROBLEM SET 6

Directions: For each question in this section, select the best answer from among the choices given and fill in the corresponding oval on the answer sheet.

Each sentence below has one or two blanks, each blank indicating that something has been omitted. Beneath the sentence are five words or sets of words labeled A through E. Choose the word or set of words that, when inserted in the sentence, <u>best</u> fits the meaning of the sentence as a whole.

Example:

> Medieval kingdoms did not become constitutional republics overnight; on the contrary, the change was -------.
>
> (A) unpopular   (B) unexpected   (C) advantageous
> (D) sufficient   (E) gradual
>
> Ⓐ Ⓑ Ⓒ Ⓓ ●

Recommended time: 3 to 4 minutes

---

1. It was obvious from the concerned look on David's face that his spendthrift habits had placed him in a ------- financial situation.

   (A) solvent
   (B) solid
   (C) global
   (D) precarious
   (E) benign

2. Some crops do not need to be replanted every spring; a grape arbor, while initially requiring intensive -------, can produce -------harvests for many years afterward without much work.

   (A) suffering . . barren
   (B) negotiation . . rich
   (C) labor . . cooperative
   (D) inertia . . forgotten
   (E) toil . . abundant

3. Henry Kissinger argued that a successful diplomat must always remain something of a -------, which is why he counseled President Nixon, known for his tough stance on communism, to normalize relations with communist China.

   (A) novice
   (B) pioneer
   (C) paradox
   (D) raconteur
   (E) sluggard

4. Although the playwright Ben Johnson was not highly regarded by most Elizabethans of his day, a few scholars of that time ------- his work and ------- many of his plays.

   (A) championed . . obliterated
   (B) disparaged . . legitimized
   (C) abetted . . destroyed
   (D) revered . . preserved
   (E) invoked . . undermined

5. Despite ------- training, the new paratroopers awaited their first jump from an airplane with -------.

   (A) paltry . . alarm
   (B) comprehensive . . assurance
   (C) extraneous . . indifference
   (D) methodical . . presumptuousness
   (E) extensive . . trepidation

6. Unfortunately, during the process of making a motion picture it sometimes happens that ------- revisions, poor casting decisions, and hasty compromises can be ------- the original intention of the authors.

(A) well-planned . . essential to
(B) ill-conceived . . detrimental to
(C) uncompromising . . divergent from
(D) meticulous . . injurious to
(E) distorted . . fundamental to

```
1 ⊂A⊃ ⊂B⊃ ⊂C⊃ ⊂D⊃ ⊂E⊃
2 ⊂A⊃ ⊂B⊃ ⊂C⊃ ⊂D⊃ ⊂E⊃
3 ⊂A⊃ ⊂B⊃ ⊂C⊃ ⊂D⊃ ⊂E⊃
4 ⊂A⊃ ⊂B⊃ ⊂C⊃ ⊂D⊃ ⊂E⊃
5 ⊂A⊃ ⊂B⊃ ⊂C⊃ ⊂D⊃ ⊂E⊃
6 ⊂A⊃ ⊂B⊃ ⊂C⊃ ⊂D⊃ ⊂E⊃
```

WORDS YOU DIDN'T KNOW FROM PROBLEM SET 6

Before you check your answers below, take a minute to write down the words you didn't know from the previous questions. Look them up and review them tomorrow.

Word   **Definition**

_____   _____

_____   _____

_____   _____

_____   _____

_____   _____

_____   _____

ANSWERS AND EXPLANATIONS: PROBLEM SET 6

There are six sentence completions in this section, so you know that the first two will be relatively easy, the second two will be medium, and the last two will be relatively difficult. Did you remember not to skip any questions?

1. **D** The clues here are the "concerned" look on David's face and the word "spendthrift" (meaning "one who spends extravagantly"). Clearly his financial position is not too good. Choice A, "solvent," in this case means "able to pay all debts," so that's wrong. Choice E, "benign," means "harmless." The correct answer is choice D, "precarious" (meaning "unstable, insecure").

2. **E** The trigger word "while" combines with the clue ("without much work") to signify that although at first a grape arbor requires -------, later it's rather easy. If the word you are thinking of is "work" or "labor," you are on just the right track. Looking at the first words in the answer choices, there are two that seem possible: choices C and E. Now, look at the second blank. Do you think the harvests are going to be described with a positive adjective or a negative adjective? You got it! You are looking for a good adjective. "Abundant" fits the bill. "Cooperative" is neither good nor bad, and makes no real sense. The correct answer is choice E.

3. **C** Kissinger advises the President to do something that seems to contradict Nixon's normal behavior. Which of these words describes contradictory behavior? Choice C, "paradox" (meaning "something that seems to contradict itself"), is the best answer. A "raconteur" is a "skilled storyteller," and a sluggard is a "person lacking energy."

4. **D** The trigger word "although" signifies that, contrary to most Elizabethans, the scholars mentioned in the second half of the sentence did like Ben Johnson. In this sentence, either blank is fine to start with, and your choice will probably be determined by whether you knew more of the vocabulary words for the first blank or for the second.

What if you don't know the meaning of a number of the possible words for either blank in the answer choices. Why not try the +/– technique? Here are the correct symbols for the missing words in the sentence and the answer choices:

...a few scholars of that time + his work and +
many of his plays.

(A) + . . –
(B) – . . +
(C) + . . –
(D) + . . +
(E) ? . . –

Choice D was the only one in which both words were positive. "Revered" means "regarded with awe," "disparaged" means "spoke disrespectfully about," "abetted" means "acted as an accomplice or aided," and "championed" means "defended or supported."

5. **E** This sentence could have gone one of two ways:

1) Despite [good] training, they awaited their jump with [fear], or
2) Despite [bad] training, they awaited their jump with [confidence].

Given the way most people feel about jumping out of an airplane, the first alternative seems more likely, and in fact, choice E gives you a clear version of that alternative. "Trepidation" means "fear." All of the other choices mix up their meanings. For example, choice A says, roughly speaking, "Despite [bad] training, they awaited their jump with [fear]," and choice B says, roughly speaking, "Despite [good] training, they awaited their jump with [confidence]."

6. **B** The first word of the sentence lets you know that the writer is not pleased with what is to follow. There is also a structural clue in the way the list of three things is presented in the middle of the sentence: ------- revisions, poor casting, and hasty compromises. What type of word do you think belongs in the blank? That's right: something negative. Only two of the answer choices begin with negative words: choices B and E.

Now, look at the second blank. How do you think all these compromises and bad casting are going to affect the "original intention" of the authors? That's right—badly. Do you want "detrimental to" or "fundamental to?" The best answer is choice B.

SENTENCE COMPLETION: PROBLEM SET 7

Directions: For each question in this section, select the best answer from among the choices given and fill in the corresponding oval on the answer sheet.

Each sentence below has one or two blanks, each blank indicating that something has been omitted. Beneath the sentence are five words or sets of words labeled A through E. Choose the word or set of words that, when inserted in the sentence, <u>best</u> fits the meaning of the sentence as a whole.

Example:

Medieval kingdoms did not become constitutional republics overnight; on the contrary, the change was -------.

(A) unpopular   (B) unexpected   (C) advantageous
(D) sufficient   (E) gradual

Ⓐ Ⓑ Ⓒ Ⓓ ●

Recommended time: 3 to 4 minutes

1. The sculptor avoided the sharp angles and geometric shapes of abstract art, instead creating ------- shapes that seemed to expand or contract as one looked at them.

   (A) static
   (B) infallible
   (C) fluid
   (D) methodical
   (E) residual

2. The initial ------- of many of the first-year law students ------- when they discover how many hours per week are necessary just to complete the course reading.

   (A) apprehensiveness . . subsides
   (B) torpor . . increases
   (C) courage . . rebounds
   (D) enthusiasm . . wanes
   (E) satisfaction . . continues

3. The graduate student's radical theories were ------- by the elder scientist because they did not ------- the elder scientist's own findings.

   (A) accepted . . confirm
   (B) discounted . . corroborate
   (C) confounded . . disprove
   (D) praised . . prove
   (E) tolerated . . support

4. Because the course was only an introduction to the fundamentals of biology, the students were surprised to be asked for such ------- information on the exam.

   (A) irrelevant
   (B) mundane
   (C) redundant
   (D) superficial
   (E) esoteric

5. Torn between a vacation in Florida and a vacation in Wyoming, Lisa ------- for several weeks.

   (A) vacillated
   (B) mitigated
   (C) terminated
   (D) speculated
   (E) repudiated

6. The lemur, a small, monkey-like animal native to Madagascar, is not, as was once mistakenly thought, a direct ------- of man; new discoveries reveal that the lemur and man once shared a common ancestor but then proceeded on ------- evolutionary paths.

   (A) relative . . converging
   (B) ancestor . . divergent
   (C) descendant . . synchronous
   (D) terrestrial . . parallel
   (E) subordinate . . similar

7. Although many believed that the problems of the community were -------, the members of the governing council refused to give in and came up with several ------- solutions.

    (A) indomitable . . ingenious
    (B) intractable . . inconsequential
    (C) exorbitant . . promising
    (D) irrelevant . . lofty
    (E) obscure . . meager

8. No detail is too small for Coach Williams when her little league team is in a playoff game, but some parents find her to be too ------- and wish that she would spend more time ------- qualities such as good sportsmanship in her young charges.

    (A) meticulous . . instilling
    (B) circumstantial . . finding
    (C) ambivalent . . impeding
    (D) conspicuous . . obstructing
    (E) ambidextrous . . thwarting

1 ⊂A⊃ ⊂B⊃ ⊂C⊃ ⊂D⊃ ⊂E⊃
2 ⊂A⊃ ⊂B⊃ ⊂C⊃ ⊂D⊃ ⊂E⊃
3 ⊂A⊃ ⊂B⊃ ⊂C⊃ ⊂D⊃ ⊂E⊃
4 ⊂A⊃ ⊂B⊃ ⊂C⊃ ⊂D⊃ ⊂E⊃
5 ⊂A⊃ ⊂B⊃ ⊂C⊃ ⊂D⊃ ⊂E⊃
6 ⊂A⊃ ⊂B⊃ ⊂C⊃ ⊂D⊃ ⊂E⊃
7 ⊂A⊃ ⊂B⊃ ⊂C⊃ ⊂D⊃ ⊂E⊃
8 ⊂A⊃ ⊂B⊃ ⊂C⊃ ⊂D⊃ ⊂E⊃

WORDS YOU DIDN'T KNOW FROM PROBLEM SET 7

Before you check your answers below, take a minute to write down the words you didn't know from the previous questions. Look them up and review them tomorrow.

Word

_____

_____

_____

_____

_____

Definition

_____

_____

_____

_____

_____

ANSWERS AND EXPLANATIONS: PROBLEM SET 7

There are 8 sentence completions in this section, so you know that the first two or three will be relatively easy, the second three or four will be medium, and the last two or three will be relatively difficult. Did you remember not to skip any questions?

1. **C** This question would be more difficult if the wrong answer choices matched the level of difficulty of the right one. "Fluid" (meaning "capable of changing") is on the Hit Parade, and it's an important word to commit to memory.

2. **D** How would you feel if you had just gotten into law school—and you had really wanted to go there? Probably pretty good. Now, how would you feel if you found out that once you were there you were going to have to put in 50 hours per week just to keep up with the reading? Probably pretty bad. That is all you need to know to answer this question.

   Initially they feel pretty [good], and then that good feeling [goes away]. Starting with the first blank, you can eliminate choices A, "apprehensiveness," and B, "torpor" (meaning "lack of energy").

   Now look at the second words in the answer choices that remain. The only one that means "goes away" is choice D, "wanes" (meaning "to decrease in size").

3. **B** The elder scientist is either going to accept or reject the student's radical theories—so which one is it going to be? The clue here is ". . . the scientist's own findings." The scientist is only human; if the student agrees with the scientist, the scientist will be more likely to accept the student's findings. If the student disagrees with the scientist, the scientist will be more likely to throw out the student's wild theories.

Look at the answer choices. Choices A, D, and E make no sense because why should the scientist "accept," "praise," or "tolerate" theories that do not "confirm," "prove," or "support" his own? Choice B seems very likely because the scientist is "discounting" (meaning "to put a reduced value on, or to ignore") theories that don't corroborate his own. (By the way, if you got this one wrong, make a note to yourself to remember secondary meanings—"discounting" does not always have to take place in a store.) Choice C implies that the scientist disliked the ideas because they agreed with his own, which doesn't make sense. "Confound" means "to confuse or perplex."

4. **E** The trigger word "because" helps a little, but the key words here are "only" and "fundamentals." Here is a slightly simplified version of the sentence: "Because the course was really basic, the students freaked out at the [hard] questions on the test." You are looking for a word like "hard." The best answer is choice E, "esoteric" (meaning "known only by a select few").

5. **A** Basically, Lisa can't make up her mind. Which of these answer choices means that? Choice A, "vacillated," means "to go back and forth," and is the correct answer. To "mitigate" means "to make milder." To "repudiate" means "to disown, or refuse to acknowledge."

6. **B** Tackle the second blank first. The lemur and man once shared a common ancestor BUT (trigger word) they then did something else. The "but" tells you that the sentence is going off in a different direction, just as apparently did the lemur and man. Which of the second words in the answer choices would indicate a new direction? There's really only one: choice B, "divergent." Just to check, look at the first blank now. In choice A, "relative" was possible, but "converging" (meaning "coming together") is the opposite of what you need. In choice C, "descendant" is wrong, because the monkey didn't evolve from man. Choice D doesn't make sense either because "terrestrial" simply means "living on the earth." In choice E, "subordinate," meaning "placed in a lower order," might be okay, but the two paths are not similar. The best answer is choice B.

7. **A** The first blank describes the community's problems, and the second blank describes the solutions. If you had to guess, the first word is going to be negative, and the second word is going to be positive. Tackle the first blank first. You need a negative word to describe problems. "Indomitable" (meaning "unable to be overcome") fits the bill, as does "intractable" (which means "not easily managed"). The other words don't really describe problems that the community refuses to give in about.

Now look at the second words in the answer choices that remain. "Ingenious" seems just right to describe solutions. "Inconsequential" (meaning "of little consequence, or importance") does not. The best answer is choice A.

8. **A** Look at the second blank. Parents think that qualities like good sportsmanship are important. Would they want the coach to "teach" these qualities in their children or "ignore" these qualities in their children? You want a word like "teach." Choices A and B provide words closest to "teach" for the second word. "Impeding," "obstructing," and "thwarting" are all negative words meaning "to prevent."

Now look at the first blank. The clue here is "No detail is too small" for the coach. However, note the trigger word "but" that follows. The parents think she is too detail-oriented. Which answer choice gives you a word like "detail-oriented" for the first blank? The best answer is choice A. "Meticulous" means "attentive to details." "Circumstantial" means "consisting only of details." "Ambidextrous" means "able to use either the right hand or the left hand equally well."

3

Short Reading

SHORT READING

Each short reading passage will consist of a brief paragraph—usually fewer than 100 words—followed by two questions. You might also see a pair of short passages followed by three or four questions. By using the approach we will show you in this chapter, you'll learn not only the best way to tackle this type of problem but also some effective strategies for eliminating wrong answers.

Let's take a look at a sample short reading passage:

Questions 1-2 are based on the following passage.

Line

       In 1782, philosopher J. Hector St. John de Crèvecoeur became the first to apply the word "melting" to a population of immigrants: "Here individuals of all nations are melted into a new
5 race of men." Crèvecoeur idealized a nation built from individuals who had transcended their origins and embraced a common American ethos: "From involuntary idleness, servile dependence, penury, and useless labour, he has passed to toils of a very different
10 nature, rewarded by ample subsistence. This is an American." While debate raged as to what exactly "melting" meant—diverse peoples coexisting peacefully while maintaining their differences or refashioning themselves to blend indistinguishably into a new,
15 common substance—Crèvecoeur's term was here to stay: America, settled by immigrants, was to have a unified populace.

Fascinating, right? Now let's figure out the best way to approach a short reading passage.

THE PRINCETON REVIEW METHOD

Step One   Read the questions first. Before you dive into the passage, take a moment to read the questions first and figure out what type of information ETS is going to ask you about. Each passage contains a huge number of facts—most of which are completely irrelevant. Don't read the passage without knowing what you're looking for.

Step Two   Read what you need. The answer to the question is contained somewhere in the passage. Read only enough of the passage to answer the question ETS asks you.

THE QUESTION TYPES

INFORMATION RETRIEVAL QUESTIONS

Many of the questions on short reading passages will require you to find specific information contained within the paragraph. Use the line references or lead words that are found in the question to jump right to the appropriate part of the passage to find the answer.

Let's return to the sample passage and take a look at question number one:

1. According to the passage, "debate raged" (line 11) over whether immigrant groups

   (A) had the ability to put their differences aside and coexist peacefully.
   (B) understood what Crèvecoeur originally meant by the term "melting."
   (C) would ultimately reject America's open immigration policy.
   (D) needed to change their identity to match an American identity.
   (E) transcended their humble origins merely by moving to America.

ETS will not always provide a line reference. If this occurs, look for a lead word—a name, a date, or a term that will stand out as you skim about the passage.

For example:

1. According to the passage, ongoing debate over Crèvecoeur's term centered primarily on whether

If ETS had asked the above question, you would use "debate" as your lead word.

In either case, your plan is the same: Locate the appropriate line reference or lead word in the passage and read a few lines before and a few lines after it. Keep reading until you find the answer to the question.

Let's go back to the passage and re-read the last sentence. Were you able to find the answer? If you said that the debate over "melting" was whether different ethnic groups would preserve their unique cultural identities and respectfully accommodate each other or whether they would create a new, common American identity, you're on the right track. Now find this paraphrase in the answer choices. The best answer is choice D.

INFERENCE QUESTIONS

The key to success on inference questions is to first understand what an inference is. An inference is a statement that must be true based on the information provided in the passage. In other words, you should never actually try to infer something in an inference question. Stick to the facts. Let's try one:

2. It can be most reasonably inferred from the passage that

   (A) debate continues to this day over whether the American ethos has changed.

   (B) people did not refer to immigrants melting into a new populace in the seventeenth century.

   (C) Crèvecoeur believed his aristocratic upbringing was a humble origin.

   (D) all Americans were able to find ample subsistence in 1782.

   (E) many immigrants moved to America because they felt useless in their country of origin.

Where should you look to find the answer to this question? While it appears that there is no line reference or lead word, there actually is. On inference questions, it's usually a good strategy to use lead words in the answer choices to help guide you to the right answers. Start with answer choice A and check the passage to see if debate *continues to this day* over the American ethos. Can you prove that answer to be true with information from the passage? If not, it cannot be the correct answer. Check the other choices. Which one is supported by the passage? The correct answer is choice B because the first sentence says that Crèvecoeur was "the first" to use the term "melting" in reference to immigrant groups. If you selected choices C, D, or E, you assumed something that wasn't stated in the passage.

MAIN IDEA QUESTIONS

Main idea questions ask you to find the point of the entire paragraph. If possible, do a main idea question after doing any inference or information retrieval questions. On main idea questions, eliminate answers that are too broad or too specific. Here's another passage and question:

Question 3 is based on the following passage.

Perhaps the scientists most excited about reigniting the lunar program are not lunar specialists, but astronomers studying a wide range of subjects. Such scientists would like
5 new missions to install a huge telescope with a diameter of 30 meters on the far side of the moon. Two things that a telescope needs for optimum operation are extreme cold and very little vibration. Temperatures on the moon can
10 be as frigid as 200 C below zero in craters on the dark side. Because there is no seismic activity, the moon is a steady base. Permanent darkness means the telescope can be in constant use. Proponents claim that under these conditions a lunar-based
15 telescope could accomplish as much in seventeen days as the replacement for the Hubble telescope will in ten years of operation.

3. The main idea of the above passage is most accurately described by which of the following statements?

(A) Most astronomers are in favor of re-igniting the lunar program.
(B) New lunar missions could discover important new features of the moon.
(C) The new lunar telescope will replace the defunct Hubble telescope.
(D) Recent discoveries have been made about weather on the dark side of the moon.
(E) Some scientists believe the moon is an ideal location for an interplanetary telescope.

A good way to tackle a main idea question is to read the first and last lines of the paragraph. From those two lines, you know that some scientists are excited about restarting the lunar program and that a lunar telescope would be very effective. Start eliminating answers right away. Choices B and D should go because they don't even mention a lunar telescope. If you're leaning towards answer choice E right now, you're on to something. You should be wary of choice A because it says "most" astronomers. Does the passage support that statement? Nope, get rid of it. Choice C makes it sound as if the telescope is already being built. But the passage doesn't state that the telescope is definitely going to be built. Thus, choice E is best.

QUICK QUIZ #1

Questions 1-2 are based on the following passage.

Line

Some historians believe that the English
Reformation actually began when Edward VI
succeeded Henry VIII. By creating the Church of
England in the 1530s, Henry VIII not only annulled his
5 marriage, but was also able to improve his bankrupt
kingdom's fortunes. By 1540, more than 500 Catholic
monasteries were closed and their wealth was
transferred to the Crown. By the time of Edward VI's
succession, the fundamental changes had been made,
10 so the new king began a campaign against iconography.
Starting in 1547, the order to remove religious icons
from places of worship was carried out. Zealous
followers of the Protestant monarch destroyed wall
paintings, statues, and shrines, effectively divesting the
15 country of most of its decorative religious art.

1. The passage most strongly implies that

   (A) by 1540, there were no monasteries left in
       England
   (B) Henry VIII was primarily interested in
       reforming the Church
   (C) Edward VI was not interested in the
       financial aspects of the Reformation
   (D) Henry VIII had secular reasons for creating
       the Church of England
   (E) Henry VIII and Edward VI shared the
       same views on marriage

2. The reference to "zealous followers"
(lines 12-13) serves primarily to indicate that

   (A) some of Edward's subjects willingly
       obeyed the King's edict
   (B) Edward's followers were apathetic about
       this campaign
   (C) the English hated decorative art at that
       time
   (D) Protestants are passionate about their
       beliefs
   (E) the Church of England condoned
       iconography

Answers and Explanations: Quick Quiz #1

1. **D** The word "implies" indicates an inference question. Choice D is correct because at least one secular reason is stated in the passage. Choice A is not supported in the passage. Watch out for choices that make extreme statements. Choices B, C, and E are incorrect because they are not mentioned in the passage.

2. **A** The passage states that the "zealous followers…destroyed" the religious art following the order to remove the icons. Choice B is the opposite of what is stated. Choice C is wrong because it generalizes that all decorative art was hated. Choice D is also a generalization; it makes a statement about present day Protestants ("are") even though the passage is about the sixteenth century. Choice E is contradicted in the passage.

OTHER QUESTION TYPES

Now let's look at some other question types that may appear. These question types don't show up as frequently as do information retrieval, inference, and main idea questions, but it is important to know how to approach them.

STRUCTURE QUESTIONS

Structure questions ask you how a particular sentence functions in the paragraph. Read the sentence in question and a sentence or two before and after it. Ask yourself "What does this sentence do?"

Questions 1-2 are based on the following passage.

	An infant's lack of sparkling dialogue may
	obscure the fact that we are all born with an ability to
Line	communicate. A capacity for language exists in our tiny,
	screaming bodies in the delivery room, along with our
5	eyes, ears, arms, legs, and vital organs. Our language
	instincts must be stimulated—we need to hear people
	talk in order to form words—but we are born eager
	to speak. The newborn baby is patiently waiting for
	answers to questions: "What will I call the objects that
10	surround me? How will I form positive and negative
	sentences? How can I express feelings about objects
	and people?" The child's brain instinctively searches
	for answers to these questions and then, like a sponge,
	soaks them up.

1. The author asks a series of questions in order to show that newborn babies

   (A) are eager to communicate
   (B) can speak certain questions
   (C) are ignorant about language
   (D) are curious about their futures
   (E) are able to teach themselves to speak

Scan the passage for question marks; then read the third, fourth, and fifth sentences. What's the point of the questions in the fourth sentence? According to the third sentence, the baby is eager to speak and is waiting for answers to questions; in the fifth sentence, the author states that the baby searches for the answers to these questions. The fourth sentence seems to be examples of questions a baby might want to ask and have answered. Which answer choice states this? Choice A is best. If you fell for choice D, be careful. All the lines mention communication, but none of them mention the future. Remember: The right answer is always stated in the passage.

VOCABULARY IN CONTEXT

These questions test your vocabulary. Luckily, you have some context to help you figure out the word. Always go back to the passage and look for clues and triggers, just as you would do for a sentence completion. Beware of Joe Bloggs trap answers!

2. In line 6, the word "stimulated" most nearly means

   (A) created
   (B) touched
   (C) aroused
   (D) encouraged
   (E) quickened

Did you pick choice C? Sorry, Joe, it's a trap. While "aroused" is one meaning of "stimulated," it's not the *right* meaning in this context. Go back to the passage and find the right answer. The clue in the third sentence is "we need to hear people talk in order to form words"—which word most closely matches this idea? "Encouraged" in choice D is best.

ARGUMENT QUESTIONS

An argument question requires you to strengthen or weaken one of the author's points. Argument questions can be tough and are good questions to skip if you can afford to.

Question 4 is based on the following passage.

The goal of plants, or any living organism, is to propagate as much as possible. To this end, many
Line plants in the wild, including wheat's ancestor, have mechanisms that scatter seeds as widely as possible.
5 However, this adaptation makes it difficult to cultivate some plants; it is impossible to farm productively if a crop is spread hither and thither! Wild wheat had a number of other mechanisms that supported its existence in nature but lessened its usefulness in the
10 field. A number of mutations had to take place before wild wheat was a suitable candidate for agriculture. Humans encouraged these mutations by providing a stable environment that favored and nurtured the mutations that would have proven deleterious in the
15 wild.

4. Which of the following would most strengthen the author's claim about the development of wheat?

(A) Scientists are now able to manipulate a plant's genes to achieve desired traits.
(B) There are presently 18 different strains of wheat being cultivated in different parts of the world.
(C) In the wild, an occasional wheat plant develops that does not spread its seeds.
(D) Wheat has an unusually stable genome, which rarely manifests any change.
(E) Wild wheat varies from domestic wheat only in an insignificant manner.

First, go back to the passage and figure out exactly which claim the question is referring to. What claim is the author making about the development of wheat? The author concludes that "humans encouraged" the mutations that would be favorable to agriculture. Now find an answer choice that would support this claim. Choice A is the best answer; it says that humans can in fact change a plant's characteristics.

Before you move on, take a look at choice D. Some argument questions ask you to weaken the author's point. If so, pick the answer that counters the author's conclusion. This author wants us to believe that humans changed the characteristics of wheat by encouraging mutations. But choice D states that, in fact, the genome of wheat doesn't change much. If this question had asked you to weaken the author's conclusion, the best answer would have been choice D.

QUICK QUIZ #2

Questions 1-2 are based on the following passage.

The Avon lady is getting a makeover. In an
effort to improve sales in the teen and young adult
market, Avon has launched a new line of cosmetics
sold by young sales representatives. For example,
5 female college students across the country are now
coordinating makeup parties in their dorm rooms to
peddle Avon's wares. Winning the loyalty and name
recognition of women between the ages of 16 and 24 is
imperative for beauty companies who hope that these
10 now-youthful customers will continue buying cosmetic
products throughout their adult lives. One challenge
faced by Avon's new campaign, however, is the fickle
nature of this demographic group and the need to keep
products fresh and enticing.

Line is marked at lines 3 and 5.

1. The primary purpose of this passage is to

   (A) describe a successful marketing strategy
       employed by Avon
   (B) provide a convincing argument for other
       companies to emulate Avon
   (C) explain why more cosmetics have recently
       been bought by teens and young adults
   (D) understand the challenging aspects of
       marketing cosmetics to young women
   (E) discuss Avon's approach for securing a
       new base of customers

2. Which of the following statements would
   most *weaken* the author's explanation for
   the targeting of young women by cosmetics
   companies?

   (A) Cosmetic sales for this demographic group
       are already on the rise.
   (B) Previous marketing campaigns aimed at
       young women have failed.
   (C) Avon's strategy has not been tested enough
       on the teen and young adult market.
   (D) There is little correlation between what
       women buy early in their lives and later
       in their lives.
   (E) Marketing aimed at younger customers
       will alienate older customers.

Answers and Explanations: Quick Quiz #2

1. **E** Choice E is the best answer. The first sentence doesn't tell you much, so take a look at the second. Now read the last sentence. It appears that Avon has a campaign to reach a new market. Choices A and C are incorrect because the passage does not mention if Avon's strategy has been successful in increasing sales among young women. Choice B is wrong because the passage is not trying to persuade other companies to do something. Choice D is incorrect since the passage mentions only one challenge.

2. **D** The author concludes that "Winning the loyalty and name recognition of women between the ages of 16 and 24 is imperative for beauty companies who hope that these now-youthful customers will continue buying cosmetic products throughout their adult lives." However, if there were little correlation between what women buy in their youth and what they buy later in life, there would be no need to target young women. The other answer choices are incorrect because they would not weaken this argument.

GUESSING AND PACING STRATEGIES FOR SHORT READING QUESTIONS

Try to do all information retrieval, inference, and main idea questions. Remember to support your answers with information from the passage. If you can't point to particular parts of the passages that makes your answers correct, don't pick them.

Process of elimination is a powerful tool on short reading passages. You should be able to eliminate at least one answer on every question. Be aggressive; the odds are in your favor if you can get rid of an answer or two. Eliminate answers that aren't mentioned in the passage or use extreme language such as "all," "always," "never," "impossible," and "only."

No matter how strange the question seems, keep in mind that the answer must be in the passage somewhere. Find it!

SHORT READING: PROBLEM SET 1

Each passage below is followed by questions based on its content. Answer the questions on the basis of what is <u>stated</u> or <u>implied</u> in the passage and in any introductory material that may be provided.

Questions 1-2 are based on the following passage.

Ben Jonson, a well-known playwright and seventeenth-century contemporary of John Donne,
Line wrote that while "the first poet in the world in some things," Donne nevertheless "for not keeping of
5   an accent, deserved hanging." Donne's generation admired the depth of his feeling, but was puzzled by his often irregular rhythm and obscure references. It was not until the twentieth century and modern movements that celebrated emotion and allusion that
10 Donne really began to be appreciated. Writers such as T. S. Eliot and W. B. Yeats admired the psychological intricacies of a poet who could one moment flaunt his earthly dalliances with his mistress and the next, wretched, implore God to "bend your force, to break,
15 blow, burn, and make me new."

1. The main idea of the passage is that

   (A) poetry is judged by different standards at different times
   (B) Jonson misjudged Donne's worth
   (C) the value of Donne's poetry was not really recognized until the twentieth century
   (D) Donne was a deeply conflicted and complex man
   (E) Donne's rough meter prevented him from being understood in his own time

2. It can be inferred from the passage that W. B. Yeats was

   (A) uninterested in meter and rhythm
   (B) a modern writer
   (C) close to T. S. Eliot
   (D) interested in imitating Donne's technique
   (E) suspicious of solely religious poets

Questions 3-4 are based on the following passage.

Astronauts have the opportunity to take photographs from unprecedented perspectives.
Line However, the fairly easy task of taking a photograph on Earth is much more arduous in space. Zero gravity
5 makes it difficult to stand still, but at least it makes it easy to move heavy camera equipment. The spacesuits and other accessories worn by astronauts prove to be very cumbersome when trying to snap the shutter. Other technicalities also make space photography less
10 than straightforward. For example, photos could be blurred by dirt on windows, and there is always the risk of damaging film due to exposure to just a small amount of radiation.

3. According to the passage, all of the following would affect space photography EXCEPT

   (A) bulky clothing and gloves
   (B) moving heavy equipment
   (C) dirty windows
   (D) film exposed to radiation
   (E) floating in zero gravity

4. It can be inferred from the passage that

   (A) experience taking photographs on Earth is not as helpful when in space
   (B) it is better to have film exposed to radiation than to have dirt on a window
   (C) the absence of gravity is the greatest challenge faced by astronauts
   (D) astronauts are envious of photographers who take photographs on Earth
   (E) opportunities to take photographs in space are more abundant than on Earth

Answers and Explanations: Problem Set 1

1. **C** The passage states that it was not until the twentieth century "that Donne really began to be appreciated." Choice A is too broad; it doesn't even mention Donne. Choice B is too narrow; the passage is not primarily about Jonson and his opinions. The passage is about Donne's poetry, not his psyche; thus choice D is incorrect. Choice E is too narrow; the passage states that several factors hindered Donne's contemporaries from fully appreciating him.

2. **B** Yeats is referenced as an example of the "modern movement" who appreciated Donne. Choice A is too extreme; while the passage suggests Yeats had other interests, it does not imply that he was uninterested in rhythm. Nothing in the passage supports any personal relation between Yeats and Eliot, so eliminate choice C. Choice D is not correct; while Yeats admired Donne, the passage does not suggest that he wished to imitate him. There is nothing in the passage to support choice E.

3. **B** Choice B is the correct answer because of the phrase "but at least it makes it easy to move heavy camera equipment." The other answer choices are all listed as challenges affecting space photography.

4. **A** The passage contrasts what is easy about taking photographs on Earth with what's difficult in space. Choice B is wrong because the passage does not say which situation is worse. Choice C is incorrect because it is too broad (it's not specific to space photography), and the passage mentions that zero gravity makes moving heavy equipment easy. Choice D is wrong because there's nothing in the passage that talks about astronauts being envious. Choice E is wrong because the passage does not compare the number of opportunities on Earth with those in space.

SHORT READING: PROBLEM SET 2

Each passage below is followed by questions based on its content. Answer the questions on the basis of what is <u>stated</u> or <u>implied</u> in the passage and in any introductory material that may be provided.

Questions 1-2 are based on the following passage.

February 9, 1964 marks an important date in American pop culture history: the Beatles performed live on *The Ed Sullivan Show*. Although the British rock group had appeared on American television twice
5 before, this particular performance was unlike any other. With more than 73 million viewers watching that night, it is not hard to understand how less than an hour of on-air time helped propel the Beatles to unprecedented international superstardom. Several
10 decades later, the audience remains one of the largest ever to watch a television program. And the inimitable band, as well as the historic date, is still commemorated for changing the music scene in America.

Line appears at left of line 3. *5* at left of line 5. *10* at left of line 10.

1. Lines 9-11 ("Several decades...television program") serve primarily to
   (A) further describe the demographic nature of the audience
   (B) emphasize the historic nature of the event
   (C) explain the popularity of *The Ed Sullivan Show*
   (D) compare the Beatles' popularity in 1964 with that of today
   (E) show the effect of television on American popular culture

2. It can be inferred from the passage that
   (A) the Beatles would have achieved great fame even without a television appearance
   (B) more than 73 million new viewers tuned in to watch the Beatles' performance
   (C) *The Ed Sullivan Show* provided a venue for musical performances in the 1960s
   (D) the Beatles are the most celebrated rock band to have achieved international fame
   (E) the Beatles' two earlier American television appearances are now forgotten

Questions 3-4 are based on the following passage.

Robert Schuman's orchestral music has been under-appreciated and misunderstood for many years by critics and audiences alike. The nineteenth-century
Line virtuoso's works for the piano are acknowledged
5 as brilliant masterworks. However, his large scale orchestral works have always suffered by comparison to those of contemporaries such as Mendelsohn and Brahms. Perhaps this is because Schuman's works should be measured with a different yardstick. His
10 works are often considered poorly orchestrated, but they actually have an unusual aesthetic. He treats the orchestra as he does the piano: one grand instrument with a uniform sound. This is so different from the approach of most composers that, to many, it has
15 seemed like a failing rather than a conscious artistic choice.

3. The author's primary purpose is to

   (A) praise Schuman for his innovative approach
   (B) re-evaluate the standing of Mendelsohn and Brahms
   (C) reassess a portion of Schuman's portfolio
   (D) reaffirm the value of the piano
   (E) examine the influence of Schuman's performances

4. The author's argument would be most *weakened* if it were true that

   (A) Schuman's piano music was overrated
   (B) Mendelsohn and Brahms wrote exceptional piano music
   (C) Mendelsohn's music was strongly influenced by that of Schuman
   (D) audiences find orchestral music easier to appreciate than piano music
   (E) most of Schuman's critics did not evaluate music based on comparisons with other composers

ANSWERS AND EXPLANATIONS: PROBLEM SET 2

1. **B** The referenced sentence mentions that the audience is still one of the largest in history. Choice A is incorrect because the passage does not describe who comprised the audience. Choice C is incorrect because the passage does not explain the general popularity of *The Ed Sullivan Show*. The passage does not compare the Beatles' popularity then and now (choice D), nor does it mention what effects television generally has on American pop culture (choice E).

2. **C** The passage mentions that at least one musical group (the Beatles) appeared on *The Ed Sullivan Show*. Choice A is wrong because you cannot come to that conclusion solely based on this passage. Choice B is incorrect because you do not know if all the viewers were new to watching the show. Choice D is too extreme ("most celebrated"). Choice E is wrong; because the earlier performances are mentioned in the passage, they aren't entirely forgotten.

3. **C** While Schuman is praised in the passage as stated in choice A, the primary purpose is to re-evaluate his orchestral works. Choices B, D, and E are not mentioned in the passage.

4. **E** Choice E is correct because the passage states that "his large scale orchestral works have always suffered by comparison to those of contemporaries such as Mendelsohn and Brahms" and that is one reason the music is "under-appreciated and misunderstood." Choices A, B, C, and E are not relevant to the author's argument; if any of them were true, they would have no bearing on critical or popular opinions of his orchestral music.

SHORT READING: PROBLEM SET 3

Each passage below is followed by questions based on its content. Answer the questions on the basis of what is <u>stated</u> or <u>implied</u> in the passage and in any introductory material that may be provided.

Questions 1-2 are based on the following passage.

Modern warfare is defined by the use of high-tech communications systems that allow military leaders to manage their forces instantaneously from thousands
Line of miles away. In contrast, because of slow-moving
5 communications systems, the greatest victory for U.S. forces during the War of 1812 actually occurred two weeks after a treaty was signed that officially ended the war. On January 8, 1815, the British, hoping to take control of Louisiana, attacked American militiamen
10 in New Orleans. In the failed attack, British casualties numbered approximately 2,000. Even though they were grossly outnumbered at the onset, only eight Americans died in the short battle. Unbeknownst to the commanders in New Orleans, the leaders of both
15 countries had already signed a peace agreement in Ghent, Belgium, on December 24, 1814.

1. According to the passage, American forces in New Orleans

   (A) turned the tide of the war and helped secure an American victory
   (B) did not abide by the Treaty of Ghent
   (C) outnumbered the British at the end of the battle
   (D) lacked communications systems
   (E) defended the city against a larger contingent of British troops

2. Which of the following best describes the structure of the passage?

   (A) A generalization is stated and then is followed by a specific example that undermines the generalization.
   (B) A present-day reality is stated and then is highlighted using a historical event as a contrasting example.
   (C) A historical era is described in terms of a significant battle.
   (D) An argument is outlined, and counterarguments are mentioned.
   (E) A diplomatic error is discussed and its implications are explained.

Questions 3-4 are based on the following passage.

Originally formed to protect Christian pilgrims on the roads to Jerusalem, the Knights Templar quickly
Line gained significant political and financial power. The Knights became early moneylenders and advisors to
5 monarchs in both Europe and the Middle East. Some historians say that the Knights' rapidly expanding power was in fact the cause of their demise. Regents, jealous of the Knights' hold over medieval politics, pressured the Pope to brand the Knights as heretics.
10 Orders to confiscate the property of the Knights and execute them arrived on October 13, a date that to this day is considered unlucky. Many historians maintain this order was the end of the Knights Templar. Some conspiracy theorists, however, say the Knights survived
15 in Scotland and constitute a secret society that is still alive today.

3. It can be inferred from the passage that

(A) the Knights Templar were interested in preventing crime, not practicing religion
(B) the Knights' actions conflicted with the Pope's politics
(C) monarchs had a financial motive in pressing for the Knights' execution
(D) the Knights are a powerful force in Scottish politics
(E) the Knights were executed to protect Christian theology

4. The tone of the passage is best described as

(A) insincere
(B) indifferent
(C) antithetical
(D) diffident
(E) objective

ANSWERS AND EXPLANATIONS: PROBLEM SET 3

1. **E** Choice E is the only choice that is clearly stated in the passage ("Even though they were grossly outnumbered…"). Choice A does not work because the war was officially over when the battle occurred and the passage does not state that the Americans won the war. Be careful with choice B; the American forces were unaware of the treaty at the time of the battle. Choice C is not stated in the passage—remember, don't assume anything. Choice D does not work because the Americans at New Orleans did not totally lack communications systems, just high-tech ones.

2. **B** Choice B works because the reality of modern warfare is stated and the Battle of New Orleans is used as an example of warfare that lacks real-time command. Nothing is undermined in the passage, therefore choice A is incorrect. Choice C is wrong because no era is described. Choice D does not work because the author is not making an argument—he's stating facts neutrally. Choice E is incorrect because there was no error in diplomacy; it just took too long for the word to spread.

3. **C** Choice C is correct; the monarchs pressured the pope to "confiscate the property of the Knights," which points to a financial motive. Choice A is extreme and unsupported by the passage. Choice B is incorrect because the Knights' power conflicted with the monarchs, not with the Pope's. Choice D uses the present tense; despite the claims of conspiracy theorists, there is no evidence that the Knights are a political force today. Choice E is wrong because the Knights were executed for political, not religious, reasons.

4. **E** For tone questions, look for support in the passage. Choice E is correct; the passage does not display particular bias for or against the Knights Templar. The author also gives balanced attention to a couple of different viewpoints on the topic, showing objectivity. Choice A is unsupported; the author never demonstrates other motives for his discussion. Choice B is too extreme—an ETS author will never be indifferent about his topic. Choice C is incorrect because the author is not making a statement that contrasts anything. It is unlikely that the author would be shy, so eliminate choice D.

SHORT READING: PROBLEM SET 4

Each passage below is followed by questions based on its content. Answer the questions on the basis of what is <u>stated</u> or <u>implied</u> in the passage and in any introductory material that may be provided.

Questions 1-2 are based on the following passage.

The term "genetic modification" refers to technology that is used to alter the genes of living organisms.
Line Genetically modified organisms are called "transgenic" if genes from different organisms are combined. The
5 most common transgenic organisms are crops of common fruits and vegetables, which are now grown in more than fifty countries. These crops are typically developed for resistance to herbicides, pesticides, and disease, as well as to increase nutritional value. Some
10 of these transgenic crops currently under development might even yield human vaccines. Along with improving nutrition and alleviating hunger, genetic modification of crops may also help to conserve natural resources and improve waste management.

1. The primary purpose of the passage is to

   (A) establish that transgenic crops are safe
   (B) provide information about transgenic crops
   (C) critique the process of genetic modification
   (D) praise the virtues of genetically modified foods
   (E) overcome opposition to genetically modified foods

2. In line 11, the word "yield" most nearly means to

   (A) surrender
   (B) drive slowly
   (C) replace
   (D) back down
   (E) produce

Questions 3-4 are based on the following passage.

Climatologists find it hard to determine if dramatic changes in weather are the result of pollution or part of a natural series of events. Modern weather records don't extend far enough back in time to map out definitive cycles. Recently climatologists have begun digging up data where historians usually tread—in ships' logs from the golden age of seafaring. England required its navy to keep records of each journey, a practice that became universal. Recording wind speed and other climatic details was essential for navigation. On the open sea this was the only way for the crew to determine its location, so readings were taken every six hours. A vast amount of weather data from around the world dating back to the mid-eighteenth century can now be compared with measurements derived from ice core samples, sunspot activity, and tree ring patterns.

Line

5

10

15

3. The phrase "where historians usually tread" is used in the passage to indicate that

(A) a centuries-old rivalry exists between climatologists and historians
(B) climatologists have been taking ships' logs out of the historians' office
(C) climatologists find valuable books alongside the historians' walking path
(D) scientists are utilizing resources typically regarded as historical rather than scientific
(E) scientists are more intrepid than historians have been in the past

4. It can be most reasonably inferred from lines 15-16 ("measurements . . . patterns.") that

(A) meteorological data of the past can be deduced from ice samples, sunspot activity, and tree rings
(B) eighteenth-century ship captains collected samples of ice and wood from around the world
(C) the yearly accumulation of ice and snow can be determined by the patterns left in tree rings
(D) only these items can give modern meteorologist clues to eighteenth-century weather
(E) scientists no longer need to use this information now that the ships' logs have been found

ANSWERS AND EXPLANATIONS: PROBLEM SET 4

1. **B** Choice B is correct because there is a lot of information with very little analysis or interpretation. Choice A is wrong because the safety of the foods is not discussed. Choice C is wrong because the process is not critiqued. Choice D is too strong when compared to choice B. Choice E is wrong because an opposing perspective is not mentioned in the passage.

2. **E** Look for the clue. The sentence before says the crops are "developed" for different purposes. Choice E is correct because "produce" is the best definition of "yield" as it used in the passage. Choices A, B, and D are valid definitions of "yield," but not appropriate in the context of the passage. Choice C is not a definition of "yield."

3. **D** Choice D is correct because the passage indicates scientists "have begun" to use this information, while historians "usually tread" among the material, indicating the information has typically been used by historians rather than by scientists. There is no evidence for any of the other answer choices.

4. **A** Choice A is correct because the newly discovered weather data is going to be compared to measurements from these three sources, implying that all the data measure the same thing. There is no evidence in the passage for choices B and C. Choice D is contradicted by the passage; the ships' logs show eighteenth-century weather. There is no evidence for choice E in the passage.

SHORT READING: PROBLEM SET 5

Each passage below is followed by questions based on its content. Answer the questions on the basis of what is <u>stated</u> or <u>implied</u> in the passage and in any introductory material that may be provided.

Questions 1-2 are based on the following passage.

Line

If you could take a picture of the soul, it might look something like the black and white photos of certain slaves and soldiers during the Civil War. They are men and women who didn't have time to look at themselves
5 or worry about their appearance, and it shows. Their faces transmit their passions and experiences and never betray their character. One photo shows a large man with a hard stare and a spiky beard that conveys fierceness. In another, a mother's wisdom can be seen
10 in the dark circles under her eyes. A child's skepticism is visible in his small, taut mouth. Somehow, their situations allowed their spirits to develop in their faces, untainted by luxury and self-examination.

1. The author argues that pictures taken during the Civil War are significant primarily because they

    (A) display people who were unaware they were being photographed
    (B) show people who were not self-conscious in front of the camera
    (C) portray unkempt, unattractive men and women
    (D) convey people who tried to express emotions for the camera
    (E) reveal that the soul is tangible and photographable

2. In line 7, the word "betray" most nearly means

    (A) contradict
    (B) reveal
    (C) compromise
    (D) attack
    (E) debase

Questions 3-4 are based on the following passage.

Line

5

10

The emotional reaction of disgust is often associated with the obdurate refusal of young children to consume certain vegetables. While such disgust may seem absurd to parents determined to supply their children with nutritious foods, scientists interested in hygienic behavior have a rational explanation. This theory contends that people have developed disgust as a protective mechanism against unfamiliar and possibly harmful objects. A recent study shows that disgust not only deters the ingestion of dangerous substances, but also dissuades people from entering potentially contagious situations. For instance, subjects of the study declared crowded railcars to be more disgusting than empty ones and lice more disgusting than wasps.

3. The primary purpose of the passage is to

(A) develop a general theory from a specific case
(B) utilize scientific evidence to prove a theory
(C) supply a logical reason for an apparently irrational action
(D) suggest a method for developing a defensive mechanism
(E) describe two functions served by the same reaction

4. According to the passage, the purpose of disgust is to

(A) prevent the ingestion of all dangerous substances
(B) protect people from wasps and other stinging insects
(C) limit overcrowding in railcars and other modes of public transportation
(D) encourage the avoidance of detrimental materials and situations
(E) give children a reason for refusing to eat nutritious foods

Answers and Explanations: Problem Set 5

1. **B** The author admires the subjects of the photos for being "untainted by luxury and self-examination." The other choices do not express this significance.

2. **B** Use the clue. The author uses the word "transmit" in the sentence. Pick the word that's closest in meaning to this word. The other choices do not reflect this meaning.

3. **C** Choice C is correct because the passage explains why children's disgust is not necessarily absurd. The passage isn't long enough to develop choice A or prove any theories in choice B, it doesn't talk about how to develop anything as in choice D, and it isn't primarily concerned with the two very similar functions of disgust as in choice E.

4. **D** Choice D is correct, as it is supported in the fourth sentence. Choice A is extreme, because disgust doesn't *prevent* the ingestion of *all* dangerous substances. Choice B contradicts the passage because people are more disgusted by lice than wasps. Choices C and E aren't supported by the passage.

4

Critical Reading

CRITICAL READING

All three Critical Reading sections on the SAT will contain critical reading passages. One of the sections will contain dual passages: two separate passages giving contrasting viewpoints on one topic. Critical reading questions are not arranged in order of difficulty like sentence completions, but are instead arranged in a rough chronological order. Usually the earlier questions refer to the beginning of the passage, and the answers to the later questions will be found toward the end of the passage.

The critical reading passages are simply longer versions of the short reading passages; everything you learned in the last chapter is applicable to these questions as well.

Try answering the two questions below, using what you've learned from the last chapter.

5. In line 14, "blotted out" most nearly means

(A) stained
(B) blemished
(C) obscured
(D) extinguished
(E) removed

6. The author mentions Sweden and Brazil in order to emphasize which point about the Krakatoa eruption?

(A) Although the eruption was devastating in Krakatoa, there were no effects felt in other parts of the word.
(B) The volcanic eruption was so powerful that it affected the climate of countries thousands of miles away.
(C) Local destruction in Krakatoa was enormous, but the destruction in Europe and South America was, if anything, greater.
(D) Brazil and Sweden had higher safety preparedness and thus escaped serious damage.
(E) The explosion would have been even more destructive had it happened today.

The eruption of Krakatoa sent clouds of ash and
dust into Earth's atmosphere to a height of 50 miles.
The Sun was blotted out entirely for two days within a
15 100-mile radius of the volcano, and Earth temperatures
as far away as Sweden and Brazil were several degrees
lower than average that year.

What do you notice? The answers to the above questions were located in
specific places in the passage, and you didn't have to read the entire passage to
get them right.

YOUR GOAL IS TO ANSWER QUESTIONS

No matter how much you read, the proctor will not be walking around the
examination room, saying, "Ah, Jessica! Excellent reading form. I'm giving you 20
extra points on your Critical Reading score." The only way you get points in SAT
Critical Reading is by correctly answering questions.

The sooner you get to the questions, the sooner you start earning points. For
example, both of the questions on the previous page could be answered without
reading the rest of the passage (which we didn't show you). In question 5, you
needed to supply a word that would fit in place of the quoted words "blotted
out." The best answer was choice C, "obscured," because the volcanic ash filled
the sky to the point that the sun's rays couldn't get through. Even if you had
read the entire passage several times and made extensive notes, the answer to this
question was based on only one thing: your understanding of this sentence in this
paragraph.

The best answer to question 6, which asked us why the author brought up
Sweden and Brazil, was choice B. In the context of this paragraph, the two countries
were mentioned to show just how powerful the eruption had been. Again, even
if you had memorized the entire passage, the only place to find the answer to this
question was right here in this paragraph.

These questions are pretty typical of the SAT in that they include either a line
reference or an identification of the paragraph in which the answer can be found.
Most of the questions in critical reading tell you where in the passage to look for
the answer. You can find the answers to the other questions because the questions
are arranged in chronological order. The answer to question number 3 will come
between the answers to questions 2 and 4.

THEY'RE TOO LONG!

Many students look at a passage of 70 to 90 lines and feel defeated at the thought of trying to keep track of a passage this long—but the situation is much better than they think. Critical reading passages are actually a series of small paragraphs like the one you just read. Each of these paragraphs has a couple of very specific questions based on it. And when you answer these questions, all you have to think about is the paragraph in question. Think of these longer critical reading passages as just a series of short reading passages, and you'll do fine.

THE PASSAGE TYPES

THE SOCIAL SCIENCE PASSAGE

This passage will be about a topic involving history, politics, economics, or sociology.

THE HUMANITIES PASSAGE

This might range from an excerpt about an artist to an essay about literature, music, or philosophy.

THE SCIENCE PASSAGE

Usually not too dry, the science passage frequently involves a discussion of a scientific discovery, a new scientific theory, or a controversy in any of the scientific fields.

THE NARRATIVE PASSAGE

Often an excerpt from a novel or short story, this type of passage frequently has actual dialogue and is often the most fun to read.

THE DUAL PASSAGE

One of the passages on your SAT will actually be two shorter passages giving two perspectives on one topic, followed by up to 13 questions. Recent dual passages have given two views of architecture in cities, two views on the jazz saxophonist Miles Davis, and two views on whether controversial books should be banned. Although the double passage is generally located in the 15-minute section of the SAT, it doesn't have to be. Wherever it is, you should tackle it in the following way:

1) Answer the questions based on the first passage.

2) Answer the questions based on the second passage.

3) Finally, answer the questions that refer to both passages.

THE PRINCETON REVIEW METHOD

Step One   Read the "blurb" (the introductory sentence which describes the passage).

Step Two   Go to the questions and figure out what parts of the passage you need to read.

Step Three   Read just what you need to find the answer and get your points. Almost every question will give you a line number or a lead word that will tell you where to look in the passage for your answer. Read just those parts, and if ETS does ask the question, it will include a line number so that you can go back and read about it as carefully as you like

NOTE: Remember that the only way to get points in critical reading is by correctly answering questions.

THE QUESTION TYPES

LINE REFERENCE AND LEAD WORD QUESTIONS

The majority of the critical reading questions will be line reference or lead word questions. In each case, the question will tell you where in the passage to look for the answer.

Line reference questions ask you about a part of the passage and tell you to which lines the question refers. These questions will look like one of the following:

> In paragraph 4, why does the author mention Harry McCallan?

> The author cites "many interesting creatures" in lines 34-36 in order to . . .

Sometimes, instead of a line or paragraph number, you will be asked about a proper name or important word that will be pretty easy to find in the passage by running your finger down the passage until you come across it.

In either case, you should look back to the passage and find the lines indicated by the question or the lines in which the lead word can be found. It's important to read a little above and a little below the line number mentioned or the line on which the lead word is, to make sure you understand the line in context. Then you need to pick the answer that best restates what the passage itself says on those lines.

From time to time, you will see a question that seems specific, even though it has neither a line reference nor a colorful word to help you find the reference in the passage. It's not a bad idea to skip a question like this until after you've answered the rest of the questions and have a better understanding of the passage. Remember, however, that the questions are arranged chronologically. If this is question 3, then the information you need to answer it will probably be found right after the information needed to answer question 2 and right before the information needed to answer question 4.

VOCABULARY-IN-CONTEXT QUESTIONS

Vocabulary-in-context questions always include line numbers and ask you to pick alternate words for the quoted word or phrase. Here's what they look like:

In line 44, "objective" most nearly means. . .

The thing to bear in mind in these questions is that ETS often picks words that have more than one meaning, and the words are generally not being used in their primary sense. For example, ETS's answer to the question above about the meaning of the word "objective" was the word "material"—certainly not the first meaning anyone would think of picking.

If you find yourself running out of time as you get to a critical reading passage then these are the questions to answer first. Not only do they take the least amount of time but they also require the smallest amount of overall knowledge of the passage.

GENERAL QUESTIONS

Usually there will be one general question per passage. It will probably look like one of the following:

The main idea of this passage is to

The primary purpose of the passage is to

The passage is best described as

The passage serves primarily to

The author uses the example of the [Krakatoa eruption] primarily to

Save the general questions for last. By the time you have answered all of the line reference and lead word questions, you will have read enough of the passage that you will probably have a good idea of the main point. If not, try going back and re-reading the opening line of each paragraph. It's a good bet that these lines will be a good paraphrase of the main idea.

PACING STRATEGIES FOR CRITICAL READING

Critical reading questions account for about half of the Critical Reading section on the SAT. But not all critical reading questions are created equally. Spend your time on the questions that you find to be the easiest. Usually, this will be the line reference and lead word questions. Skip any oddball questions or any questions that are difficult to understand.

If you're shooting for a top score, you should attempt all the critical reading questions. By using process of elimination, you should be able to always eliminate an answer choice or two. Once you've done that, you can and should guess. Remember that the answer to even the weirdest question is still somewhere in the passage, so if you have time left over at the end of the test go back to any questions you've skipped and comb the passage for the correct answer.

CRITICAL READING CHECKLIST

1. Read the beginning blurb.

2. Answer the line reference and lead word questions. Remember to read above and below the specified lines to understand their context. For other specific questions that don't have a line reference, use chronology to figure out where the answer will be found in the passage.

3. Answer the vocabulary-in-context questions.

4. Answer any general questions.

5. With dual passages, read the first passage first, and answer all questions relating to that passage. Then read the second passage and answer all questions related to that passage. Finally, do the questions related to both passages. These are always at the end.

CRITICAL READING: PRACTICE PASSAGE 1

Each passage below is followed by questions based on its content. Answer the questions on the basis of what is <u>stated</u> or <u>implied</u> in the passage and in any introductory material that may be provided.

Questions 1-7 are based on the following passage.

The following passage gives a critical overview of the work of Frank Lloyd Wright, one of America's most famous architects.

It is 30 years since Frank Lloyd Wright died
at 91, and it is no exaggeration to say that the
United States has had no architect even roughly
Line comparable to him since. His extraordinary 72-
5 year career spanned the shingled Hillside Home
School in Wisconsin in 1887 to the Guggenheim
Museum built in New York in 1959.
His great early work, the prairie houses of
the Midwest in which he developed his style
10 of open, flowing space, great horizontal panes,
and integrated structure of wood, stone, glass,
and stucco were mostly built before 1910. Philip
Johnson once insulted Wright by calling him
"America's greatest nineteenth-century architect."
15 But Mr. Johnson was then a partisan of the sleek,
austere International Style which Wright abhorred.
Now, the International Style is in disarray, and
what is significant here is that Wright's reputation
has not suffered much at all in the current
20 antimodernist upheaval.
One of the reasons that Wright's reputation
has not suffered too severely in the current
turmoil in architectural thinking is that he spoke
a tremendous amount of common sense. He was
25 full of ideas that seemed daring, almost absurd,
but which now in retrospect were clearly right.
Back in the 1920s, for example, he alone among
architects and planners perceived the great effect
the automobile would have on the American
30 landscape. He foresaw "the great highway
becoming, and rapidly, the horizontal line of a new
freedom extending from ocean to ocean," as he
wrote in his autobiography of 1932. Wright wrote
approvingly of the trend toward decentralization,
35 which hardly endears him to today's center-city-
minded planners—but if his calls toward suburban
planning had been realized, the chaotic sprawl of
the American landscape might today have some
rational order to it.
40 Wright was obsessed with the problem of the
affordable house for the middle-class American.

It may be that no other prominent architect has
ever designed as many prototypes of inexpensive
houses that could be mass-produced; unlike most
45 current high stylists, who ignore the boredom
of suburban tract houses and design expensive
custom residences in the hope of establishing a
distance between themselves and mass culture,
Wright tried hard to close the gap between the
50 architectural profession and the general public.
In his modest houses or his grand ones, Wright
emphasized appropriate materials, which might
well be considered to prefigure both the growing
preoccupation today with energy-saving design
55 and the surge of interest in regional architecture.
Wright, unlike the architects of the International
Style, would not build the same house in
Massachusetts that he would build in California;
he was concerned about local traditions, regional
60 climates, and so forth. It is perhaps no accident
that at Wright's Scottsdale, Arizona home and
studio that continues to function, many of the
younger architects have begun doing solar designs
as a logical step from Wright's work.

1. The phrase "comparable to" (line 4) most nearly means

   (A) as good as
   (B) similar to
   (C) like
   (D) related to
   (E) associated with

2. According to the passage, Wright's typical style included all of the following EXCEPT

   (A) the integrated use of different types of building materials
   (B) open flowing spaces
   (C) large horizontal panes
   (D) solar-powered heating systems
   (E) regional architectural elements

3. Philip Johnson's quotation about Wright (line 14) was an insult because

(A) Wright did not respect Johnson's opinion
(B) Johnson was a rival architect who wanted the title for himself
(C) it ignored the many famous buildings that Wright built in the twentieth century
(D) Johnson's International Style has since fallen out of favor
(E) Wright was an elderly man and deserved to be treated with more respect

4. In the third paragraph, the author mentions Wright's thoughts about the importance of the automobile primarily to illustrate

(A) the general mood of the times
(B) Wright's ability to correctly predict the future
(C) the absurdity of Wright's ideas
(D) the need for centralization in America
(E) Wright's somewhat egotistical demeanor

5. According to the passage, Wright foresaw that "the great effect" of the automobile (lines 28-30) would be to

(A) increase the number of highways in America
(B) enhance the need for solar-powered designs
(C) create decentralized suburban communities
(D) reduce the number of city planners
(E) weaken the International Style, an architectural movement of which Wright disapproved

6. In lines 45-46, the phrase "who ignore the boredom of suburban tract houses" most closely means the architects

(A) find these houses to be in bad taste
(B) are sympathetic to the plight of the poor
(C) are willing to overlook the financial limitations of designing houses that could be mass-produced
(D) design expensive, stylized homes for the masses
(E) do not want to be bothered with designing inexpensive homes

7. Wright's refusal to build an identical house in both Massachusetts and California (lines 56-58) came out of his conviction that

(A) each house should be a unique design, never to be duplicated
(B) only International Style homes could be duplicated anywhere
(C) each design should reflect features of regional architecture and climate concerns
(D) he would design only for midwestern locations
(E) although he designed homes for mass production, he felt others should do the actual duplication

```
1 ⊂A⊃  ⊂B⊃  ⊂C⊃  ⊂D⊃  ⊂E⊃
2 ⊂A⊃  ⊂B⊃  ⊂C⊃  ⊂D⊃  ⊂E⊃
3 ⊂A⊃  ⊂B⊃  ⊂C⊃  ⊂D⊃  ⊂E⊃
4 ⊂A⊃  ⊂B⊃  ⊂C⊃  ⊂D⊃  ⊂E⊃
5 ⊂A⊃  ⊂B⊃  ⊂C⊃  ⊂D⊃  ⊂E⊃
6 ⊂A⊃  ⊂B⊃  ⊂C⊃  ⊂D⊃  ⊂E⊃
7 ⊂A⊃  ⊂B⊃  ⊂C⊃  ⊂D⊃  ⊂E⊃
```

ANSWERS AND EXPLANATIONS: PRACTICE PASSAGE 1

As you read the passage, you looked for the main idea of the passage and a general sense of what goes on in the individual paragraphs. The italicized introductory material told you this would be an overview of the work of a famous architect, but it was not until you read the first paragraph that you knew how the author felt about Wright: The first paragraph could be summarized as "Wright is great!" The second paragraph is devoted to his early work. The third paragraph is about his common sense and his foresight. The fourth paragraph concerns his attempts to design affordable homes for the middle class. The fifth paragraph speaks of how his designs prefigured today's concerns with regional architecture and energy-saving design.

Now, attack the questions.

1. **A** From the blurb, you know that this passage is basically about the famous architect. Reading the entire sentence in which the quoted word appears, it's clear the author says that no other architect has come close to being as good as Wright. Thus, it is not enough to use the words in choices B or C. You need something stronger. Choices D and E, which merely say there have been no architects connected to Wright, seem both factually incorrect (based on what you learn later in the passage) and inconsistent with the intended meaning of the sentence. The best answer is choice A.

2. **D** You may have initially skipped this question because it did not contain a line reference, while many of the other questions did. However, this being the second question, you can assume that the answer will be found somewhere near the beginning of the passage. In this case, the answers (correct and incorrect) can be found in lines 8-12 at the beginning of the second paragraph.

   Remember that this is an EXCEPT question, so look for the one answer that is NOT true. Choices A, B, and C were easy to find in the lines just mentioned. Choices D and E seem less obvious. Did Wright's homes use solar power? Much later in the passage, the author says that his later disciples used solar power in their designs as a kind of logical extension of Wright's principles, but nowhere is it stated that Wright himself used solar heating. Wright's taste for regional elements is spoken of later as well, but you get a good hint of this in the lines already cited, where the author speaks of Wright's "prairie houses of the Midwest." The best answer is choice D.

3. **C** This question is a little tough because the answer is not completely spelled out. In the previous paragraph you had been told that Wright designed buildings from the 1880s through at least 1959 when he designed the famous Guggenheim Museum. Obviously, most of his designs were done during the twentieth century. Thus, Johnson put Wright down by implying that his only important work had taken place very early in his career.

Because this was a subtle point, you may have been better off eliminating incorrect answer choices.

(A)   If Wright really didn't respect Johnson's opinion, then he wouldn't have been very insulted by Johnson's comment.

(B)   The fact that Johnson was a jealous rival would not explain why his seeming compliment was in fact an insult.

(D)   Why would what later happened to Johnson's movement have anything to do with his statement being an insult?

(E)   This is a possible answer, but you actually have no way of knowing when Johnson made the statement—Wright might still have been a relatively young man when it was made.

> **Read a few lines above and below the quoted lines to understand the context.**

4. **B** As always, you should read the paragraph not only for the sentences related to the automobile, but for the context in which those sentences are presented. A bit earlier in the paragraph, the author says, "He was full of ideas that seemed daring, almost absurd, but (*trigger word*) which now in retrospect were clearly right." The automobile sentences are presented as an example of Wright's foresight. The correct answer is choice B. Choice A is a little too vague. If you selected choice C, you missed the trigger word. Choice D gets the meaning wrong: Wright favored decentralization. If you selected choice E, you might well have been correct about his demeanor, but you didn't get it from this passage. Be careful about outside information.

5. **C** It's always great when two questions refer to the same patch of passage—you've just been reading and thinking about these sentences in order to answer question 4. The beginning of the sentence that contained the quote stated, "…he alone among architects and planners perceived…." Thus, he thought about these issues as an architect. What relevance could the expansion away from cities have on an architect? This expansion would lead to an expansion of suburban communities. This is spelled out further toward the end of the paragraph. Choice A would have little effect on an architect. Choice B speaks of a design that was not possible during Wright's lifetime. Choices D and E might both be true, but neither was stated in the passage. The correct answer is choice C.

6. **E** In this paragraph, Wright is set in opposition to most current architects. Note the trigger word in the following sentence: "Unlike (*trigger word*) most current high stylists, who ignore the boredom of suburban tract houses…, Wright tried hard to close the gap between the architectural profession and the general public." Wright designed for the common person; most current architects do not. Thus choices B, C, and D can be eliminated—D because the masses can't afford expensive homes. Choice A got these architects' distaste right, but didn't catch the intention of the passage to portray them as not wishing to get involved in the business of mass-produced homes. The best answer is choice E.

7. **C** The answer to this question came from the sentences immediately before and immediately after the quoted lines. "Local traditions and regional climates" were Wright's reasons for not duplicating houses in different parts of the country.

CRITICAL READING: PRACTICE PASSAGE 2

Each passage below is followed by questions based on its content. Answer the questions on the basis of what is <u>stated</u> or <u>implied</u> in the passage and in any introductory material that may be provided.

Questions 1-7 are based on the following passage.

Many articles and books have been written proposing a major revamping of the nation's school system. In this excerpt, the author presents his own views on this subject.

When nearly everybody agrees on something, it probably isn't so. Nearly everybody agrees: It's going to take a revolution to fix America's public
Line schools. From the great national think tanks to the
5 neighborhood PTA, the call to the barricades is being trumpeted. Louis V. Gerstner Jr., head of RJR Nabisco and one of the business leaders in education reform, proclaims the Noah Principle: "No more prizes for predicting rain. Prizes only for building
10 arks. We've got to change whole schools and the whole school system."

But it isn't so; most of that is just rhetoric. In the first place, nobody really wants a revolution. Revolution would mean junking the whole present
15 structure of education overnight and inventing a new one from scratch, in the giddy conviction that anything must be an improvement—no matter what it costs in terms of untaught kids, wrecked careers, and doomed experiments. What these folks really
20 want isn't revolution but major reform, changing the system radically but in an orderly fashion. The changes are supposed to be tested in large-scale pilot programs—Gertner's "arks"—and then installed nationally.
25 But even that is just a distant gleam in the eye and a dubious proposition too. There's nothing like a consensus even on designing those arks, let alone where they are supposed to come to ground. And anyone who has watched radical reforms in the real
30 world has to be wary of them: Invariably, they take a long time and cost a great deal, and even so they fail more often than they succeed. In organizations as in organisms, evolution works best a step at a time. The best and most natural changes come not
35 in wholesale gulps, but in small bites.

What the think-big reformers fail to acknowledge is that schools all over the country are changing all the time. From head-start programs to after-school big brother/big sister projects to self-
40 esteem workshops, it's precisely these small-scale innovations and demonstration programs that are doing the job, in literally thousands of schools. Some of these efforts are only partly successful; some

fail; some work small miracles. They focus varyingly
45 on children, teacher, and parents, on methods of administration and techniques of teaching, on efforts to motivate kids and to teach values and to mobilize community support. Some are relatively expensive; others cost almost nothing. But all of them can be
50 done—and have been done.

The important thing is that local schools aren't waiting for a revolution, or for gurus to decree the new model classroom from sea to shining sea. They are working out their own problems and making
55 their own schools better. And anyone—teachers, parents, principals, school board members—anyone who cares enough and works hard enough can do the same.

1. The primary purpose of the passage is to

   (A) present an alternative view on a widely-held belief
   (B) refute the notion that change of any kind is needed
   (C) describe several plans to implement an educational revolution
   (D) uncover and analyze new flaws in an old system
   (E) relate the historical events that have shaped a situation

2. The quotation in lines 8-10 ("No more prizes... arks.") can best be interpreted to mean that Gerstner believes

   (A) the present school system is functioning adequately
   (B) rather than focus on describing problems, the emphasis should be shifted to finding solutions
   (C) the author of the passage is a religious person
   (D) school curriculum should include more classes on topics such as shipbuilding, and fewer classes on meteorology
   (E) in the value of monetary prizes to outstanding students

3. The author views the pilot programs mentioned in lines 21-35 as which of the following?

> I. Costly and time-consuming
> II. A product of consensus
> III. Uncertain to succeed

(A) I only
(B) II only
(C) III only
(D) I and III only
(E) I, II, and III

4. In line 35, "wholesale" most nearly means

(A) cheap
(B) fair
(C) large
(D) valuable
(E) intensive

5. Which best summarizes the idea of "small bites" (line 35)?

(A) Changing the system radically but in an orderly fashion
(B) Making the system gradually look more like it did in the past
(C) Allowing children to choose from a variety of programs
(D) Teaching the theory of evolution in the classroom
(E) Using modest innovations to improve schools

6. According to the author, the "small-scale innovations" referred to in lines 40-41

(A) are largely theoretical so far
(B) are producing a revolution in education
(C) have in many cases been shown to work
(D) do not work on a large scale
(E) are unavailable in many areas

7. Judging from the author's discussion, he believes that local schools

(A) should embrace sweeping plans for national educational reform
(B) are relatively expensive
(C) can be only as good as their curricula
(D) are producing small but useful innovations all the time
(E) will fall victim to doomed experiments

1 ⊂A⊃ ⊂B⊃ ⊂C⊃ ⊂D⊃ ⊂E⊃
2 ⊂A⊃ ⊂B⊃ ⊂C⊃ ⊂D⊃ ⊂E⊃
3 ⊂A⊃ ⊂B⊃ ⊂C⊃ ⊂D⊃ ⊂E⊃
4 ⊂A⊃ ⊂B⊃ ⊂C⊃ ⊂D⊃ ⊂E⊃
5 ⊂A⊃ ⊂B⊃ ⊂C⊃ ⊂D⊃ ⊂E⊃
6 ⊂A⊃ ⊂B⊃ ⊂C⊃ ⊂D⊃ ⊂E⊃
7 ⊂A⊃ ⊂B⊃ ⊂C⊃ ⊂D⊃ ⊂E⊃

ANSWERS AND EXPLANATIONS: PRACTICE PASSAGE 2

1. **A** This general question asks you for the main idea of the passage—which you probably figured out while answering the other questions. In this case, the blurb tells you everything you need to know: You are told that the author presents an alternate view. To confirm this, look at the first paragraph; it tells you what "everybody agrees about." Then, in the second paragraph, after the trigger word "but," you find out what the author thinks instead. Choice B is contrary to the passage itself. No large-scale programs are described in the passage, so choice C can be eliminated. Choices D and E are also somewhat contrary to the intent of the passage. The best answer is choice A.

2. **B** As always, when ETS gives you specific lines to look at, you should remember to read above and below the quote to get a sense of the purpose of the entire paragraph. The paragraph as a whole describes what "everybody" thinks they want: a revolution in the way children are taught. Gerstner is quoted as representing this feeling. Thus choice A can be eliminated immediately; Gerstner wants radical change. It is unclear whether Gerstner is even aware of the author's existence, thus choice C is impossible. Choices D and E take the quotation too literally. Gerstner is making a metaphorical point. The best answer is choice B.

3. **D** While the pilot programs are mentioned at the end of paragraph 2, the answer to this question comes at the beginning of paragraph 3. In lines 30–32, the author says, ". . .they take a long time and cost a great deal, and even so they fail more often than they succeed." A bit earlier in the paragraph, she says, "there's nothing like a consensus even on designing those arks, let alone . . ."

    Look at the choices. Roman numeral I was definitely said, so eliminate any answer choice that does not include I. Choices B and C bite the dust. Roman numeral II gets the author's thoughts backward, so eliminate any choice that includes II; choice E can be crossed off. Roman numeral III was also definitely stated, so the best answer is choice D.

4. **C** Specific line vocabulary questions are normally quick to do, but as always, beware of secondary and far-fetched definitions. In other contexts, "wholesale" might mean cheap or fair, but in this case, the best answer is choice C. You can get this from the context of the rest of the sentence: "Not in ------- gulps, but in *small* bites."

5. **E** The answer to this question can be found in paragraph 4, lines 40–42: ". . . it's precisely these small-scale innovations. . .that are doing the job. . . ." You might not have realized where you needed to look to find this answer, but you could have eliminated several of the answer choices anyway. Because the author does not favor revolution, you can eliminate choice A. Because the author proposes small changes, you can eliminate choice B. Choice C is not mentioned in the passage at all. Choice D is a trap answer for anyone who noticed the word evolution right in front of the quoted lines. However, the author writes of the "evolution" of the school system, not evolution as it is taught (or not taught) in the schools. The best answer is choice E.

6. **C** You may have noticed that questions 5, 6, and 7 all referred to the same paragraph, which is great! By now, you must be an expert on paragraph 4. Reading from the beginning of the paragraph in which the quoted words appear, you see that "schools. . .are changing all the time." Then a bit later, you see that "it's precisely these small-scale innovations. . . that are doing the job in . . . thousands of schools. . . ." Thus, the innovations are not theoretical (cross off choice A), revolutionary (cross off choice B), or unavailable in many areas (cross off choice E). You don't have any information on whether they will work on a large scale, so the best answer is choice C.

7. **D** Because this question did not have a specific line number, you may have initially skipped it. However, if you had looked toward the end of the passage for the lead words, "local schools," the answer was to be found at the beginning of the fourth paragraph. "Schools all over the country are changing all the time." Choice A is clearly against the author's stated preference. Choices B and C are not mentioned in the passage. Choice E is a trap answer based on language in paragraph 2. The best answer is choice D.

CRITICAL READING: PRACTICE PASSAGE 3

Each passage below is followed by questions based on its content. Answer the questions on the basis of what is <u>stated</u> or <u>implied</u> in the passage and in any introductory material that may be provided.

Questions 1-7 are based on the following passage.

Scientists, theologians, and lay persons have debated the origins of life on Earth for hundreds of years. The following passage presents one scientist's explanation.

How did the earliest, most primitive, forms of life begin? Let's start with the formation of Earth 4.5 billion years ago. We can allow the first few
Line hundred million years to pass while Earth settles
5 down to more or less its present state. It cools down and squeezes out an ocean and an atmosphere. The surrounding hydrogen is swept away by the solar wind, and the rain of meteors out of which Earth was formed dwindles and virtually ceases.
10 Then, perhaps 4,000 million years ago, Earth is reasonably quiet and the period of "chemical evolution" begins. The first live molecules are small ones made up of two to five atoms each—the simplest form of life we can imagine—a single-
15 strand RNA molecule.

Different scientific theories have been proposed as to how this molecule first came into being. In 1908 the Swedish chemist Svante August Arrhenius theorized that life on Earth began when
20 spores (living, but capable of very long periods of suspended animation) drifted across space for millions of years, perhaps until some landed on our planet and were brought back to active life by its gentle environment.
25 This is highly dramatic, but even if we imagine that Earth was seeded from another world, which, long, long before, had been seeded from still another world, we must still come back to some period when life began on some world through spontaneous
30 generation—and we may as well assume that this generation began on Earth.

Why not? Even if spontaneous generation does not (or, possibly, cannot) take place on Earth now, conditions on the primordial Earth were so different
35 that what seems a firm rule now may not have been so firm then.

What won't happen spontaneously may well happen if energy is supplied. In the primordial Earth, there were energy sources—volcanic heat,
40 lightning, and most of all, sunshine. At that time, Earth's atmosphere did not contain oxygen, or its derivative, ozone, and the Sun's energetic ultraviolet rays would reach Earth's surface undiluted.

In 1954 a chemistry student, Stanley Lloyd Miller,
45 made a fascinating discovery that shed light on the passage from a substance that is definitely unliving to one that is, in however simple a fashion, alive. He began with a mixture of water, ammonia, methane, and hydrogen (materials he believed to have been
50 present on Earth at its beginning). He made sure his mixture was sterile and had no life of any kind in it. He then circulated it past an electric discharge (to mimic the energy sources roiling the planet at that time.) At the end of a week, he analyzed his
55 solution and found that some of its small molecules had been built up to larger ones. Among these larger molecules were glycine and alanine, the two simplest of the twenty amino acids. This was the first proof that organic material could have been
60 formed from the inanimate substances that existed on Earth so long ago.

1. In the first paragraph, the author discusses the "first few hundred million years" after Earth was formed in order to

   (A) illustrate two theories as to how Earth was created
   (B) demonstrate how hardy living organisms had to be to survive this initial period
   (C) describe Earth as it was before life began
   (D) discredit the theory that life had an extra-terrestrial origin
   (E) explain the concept of spontaneous generation

2. The author most likely views the theories of Svante August Arrhenius as

   (A) innovative and daring
   (B) dramatic but logical
   (C) interesting but unlikely
   (D) impossible and illogical
   (E) lunatic and unscientific

3. The word "generation" in line 30 most nearly means

   (A) descendants
   (B) development
   (C) offspring
   (D) designation
   (E) period

4. According to the passage, the "energy" mentioned in lines 37-43 may have been important for which of the following reasons?

   (A) Sources of energy found at that time produced the oxygen in Earth's atmosphere.
   (B) This energy may have helped to promote spontaneous generation.
   (C) It was more powerful than volcanic heat and ultraviolet rays at that time.
   (D) Ultraviolet energy converted oxygen into ozone.
   (E) It mimicked exactly the energy of electric discharge.

5. In line 43, the word "undiluted" most nearly means

   (A) purified
   (B) condensed
   (C) watered down
   (D) unweakened
   (E) untested

6. The author uses the example of Stanley Miller's experiment primarily to suggest

   (A) a laboratory confirmation of the theoretical possibility of spontaneous generation
   (B) the need for further research in this field
   (C) a discovery of the list of materials that were present when Earth was first created
   (D) that amino acids are not, in fact, building blocks of organic materials
   (E) the possibility of an extraterrestrial source for the first organic matter on Earth

7. The author's conclusion at the end of the last paragraph would be most directly supported by additional information concerning

   (A) what other chemical materials were present on Earth 4 billion years ago
   (B) why life did not begin during the first few hundred million years after Earth formed
   (C) whether other chemistry professors were able to re-create the same results attained by Miller
   (D) how Arrhenius went about his search for spores in meteorites
   (E) why hydrogen in Earth's atmosphere was removed by solar wind

1	⊂A⊃	⊂B⊃	⊂C⊃	⊂D⊃	⊂E⊃
2	⊂A⊃	⊂B⊃	⊂C⊃	⊂D⊃	⊂E⊃
3	⊂A⊃	⊂B⊃	⊂C⊃	⊂D⊃	⊂E⊃
4	⊂A⊃	⊂B⊃	⊂C⊃	⊂D⊃	⊂E⊃
5	⊂A⊃	⊂B⊃	⊂C⊃	⊂D⊃	⊂E⊃
6	⊂A⊃	⊂B⊃	⊂C⊃	⊂D⊃	⊂E⊃
7	⊂A⊃	⊂B⊃	⊂C⊃	⊂D⊃	⊂E⊃

Answers and Explanations: Practice Passage 3

1. **C** You know from the introductory blurb that the passage will be about a theory that explains the origin of life on Earth, not the origin of the Earth itself. Certainly there were not two theories presented. Thus eliminate choice A. Choice B, while seemingly plausible, is wrong because even the beginnings of primitive life on Earth do not start until later, according to the second paragraph. Choice C correctly describes the purpose of this description: to set the scene for the "chemical evolution" that was about to begin. Extraterrestrial origins were not brought up until the third paragraph, so eliminate choice D. If you selected choice E, you were thinking too much. Ultimately, the entire passage is helping to explain spontaneous generation, but the specific purpose of paragraph 1 is best described by choice C.

2. **C** Where do you find Arrhenius? Paragraph 3—but the author's reaction to Arrhenius is in paragraph 4. The trigger word ("but") in the middle of the first sentence tells us that the author does not totally buy Arrhenius's theory, which gets rid of choices A and B. On the other hand, does the author think he's a crackpot? No, so get rid of choices D and E. The best answer is choice C.

3. **B** Specific line vocabulary questions are easy in that you know right where to look, and you don't have to read much beyond the sentence before and after the quoted word. But they're tough in that the definitions are not always exactly what you'd expect and often entail secondary meanings. For example, here the word "generation" can mean descendants or offspring or even possibly period—but none of these is right in this case. The "generation" that's being talked about is "spontaneous generation" as it is discussed in this passage: the starting spark of primitive life where none existed before. Choice B is the best answer.

4. **B** The entire passage is about the origin of primitive life on Earth. The paragraph in question describes how this spontaneous generation might happen—by the application of various kinds of energy. If you didn't notice this while you were doing the question, you still could have eliminated a few of the other answer choices:

    (A) It was the lack of oxygen at that time that helped to let one form of energy (ultraviolet rays from sunlight) through to the surface of the planet. Eliminate.

    (C) The energy referred to in the question included volcanic heat and ultraviolet rays. Cross it off.

    (D) The paragraph didn't say this. Cross it off.

    (E) Just the opposite—the electric discharge described in the next paragraph was used by Miller to mimic the primordial energy. Eliminate.

    The best answer is choice B.

5. **D** Oxygen and ozone in Earth's atmosphere dilute the sun's rays so that they are less powerful. Four billion years ago, there was no oxygen or ozone, and so these rays were not weakened. The best answer is choice D.

6. **A** There is no line number here, but by scanning for the lead words "Stanley Miller" you will find the answer in the last paragraph. The topic sentence of the paragraph gives it all away: " . . . Miller made a fascinating discovery that shed light on the passage from a substance that is definitely unliving to one that is, in however simple a fashion, alive." His experiment helped to confirm the explanation of the origins of primitive life (spontaneous generation) that the author describes in this passage. The best answer is choice A. You could eliminate choice B because, while there is always a need for further research, this need was not mentioned at all in the passage. Miller's choice of materials may have been based on a new discovery, but again this was not the central point of the passage, so cross off choice C. Choice D contradicts the author. Miller's experiment tends to contradict choice E: Miller tried to recreate the chemicals and the energy that existed on Earth at that time.

7. **C** Miller's results wouldn't be worth much unless they could be corroborated, and this was why choice C is best. Choices B, D, and E addressed issues that were brought up in earlier paragraphs, and had little bearing on spontaneous generation. It might be interesting to know what other chemicals were present, but as long as these chemicals were present, then the experiment is valid. The best answer is choice C.

CRITICAL READING: PRACTICE PASSAGE 4

Each passage below is followed by questions based on its content. Answer the questions on the basis of what is <u>stated</u> or <u>implied</u> in the passage and in any introductory material that may be provided.

Questions 1-6 are based on the following passage.

The following passage is an excerpt from a memoir written by writer John Burke, about the novelist Joseph Heller.

I became a fan of Joseph Heller's writing while I was a student in high school in the 1970s. His most famous book, *Catch-22*, was practically an anthem
Line for my friends and me. We had dissected it, sitting in
5 the park outside school, reciting certain key passages aloud and proclaiming to anyone who would listen that this was quite possibly the best book ever written. Nearly twenty years later I am not sure that we were wrong.
10　Heller created a modern-day anti-hero who was a soldier trying to stay sane in the midst of a war in which he no longer believed. This spoke to my generation, growing up as we did during the turmoil of Vietnam, and—however you felt about the issue—
15 his ideas were considered important.
　I had spent many hours imagining what the man who had created the savage wit and brilliant imagery of that book would be like in person. I was soon to find out. To this day, I have no idea how it
20 was arranged, but somehow an invitation to speak at my high school was extended and duly accepted.
　On the day, I made sure to be near the gate of the school to see him arrive. I was looking for a limousine, or perhaps an entourage of reporters
25 surrounding the man whose dust-jacket picture I had scrutinized so often. But suddenly, there he was, completely alone, walking hesitantly toward the school like just a normal person. He walked by me, and I was amazed to see that he was wearing rather
30 tattered sneakers, down at the heel.
　When he began speaking in the auditorium, I was dumbfounded, for he had a very heavy speech impediment.
　"That can't be him," I whispered loudly to a
35 friend. "He sounds like a dork."
　My notions of a brilliant man at that time did not extend to a speech impediment—or any handicap whatsoever. Ordinary people were handicapped, but not men of brilliance. There was, in fact, a fair
40 amount of whispering going on in the auditorium.
　And then somehow, we began to listen to what he was saying. He was completely brilliant. He seemed to know just what we were thinking and articulated

feelings that I had only barely known that I had. He
45 spoke for forty minutes and held us all spell-bound. I would not have left my seat even if I could.
　As I listened, I began to feel awaken in me the possibility of being more than I had supposed that I could be. With some difficulty I managed to get to
50 the school gate again and waited for twenty minutes while I suppose he signed autographs and fielded questions inside the auditorium. Eventually, he came out, as he had come in, alone.
　I screwed up all my courage and called to him,
55 "Mr. Heller."
　He almost didn't stop but then he turned around and came over to me.
　"I just wanted to say how much I enjoyed your book. "
60　He looked down at me in my wheelchair, smiled as if it was the most normal thing in the world and shook my hand. I think that day may have been very important in the future direction of my life.

1. To the author, Joseph Heller's novel, *Catch-22* was

　(A) an important but little-known work
　(B) unusual in its frank portrayal of high school students and their problems
　(C) too traditional for most readers
　(D) inspiring and thought-provoking
　(E) more suited to an older generation

2. The major purpose of the passage is to

　(A) describe an event that may have changed the author's perception of himself
　(B) profile a famous novelist
　(C) relate in dramatic form the author's early childhood memories
　(D) suggest the sense of disappointment the author felt at encountering his hero in person
　(E) discuss the literary significance of Heller's most famous novel

3. The description of Heller's sneakers in lines 28-30 provides all of the following EXCEPT

(A) a contrast between the actual appearance of Heller and the author's image of him
(B) a telling detail about Joseph Heller
(C) a revealing insight into the mind of the author at that time
(D) a suggestion that Heller may have been dressing down deliberately to put his young audience at ease
(E) information to suggest that Heller had owned the sneakers for some time

4. The author describes Heller's speech (lines 31-46), primarily in order to

(A) illustrate the wit and imagery of the novelist's ideas
(B) describe the disappointment of the high school kids at the inarticulateness of the speaker
(C) respond to charges that Heller's work is overrated
(D) show that the students' initial skepticism was overcome by their interest in what he was saying
(E) demonstrate the lack of respect that was shown to the novelist because of his speech impediment

5. In line 51, "fielded" most nearly means

(A) evaded
(B) asked
(C) responded to
(D) delved into
(E) caught

6. The author most likely remembers his handshake with Heller because

(A) Heller almost didn't stop to shake his hand
(B) it was a form of recognition from someone who had overcome his own obstacles
(C) the author was a genuine fan of Heller's most famous book
(D) the author had been so unimpressed by Heller's speech at his high school
(E) Heller had taken the time to come to visit a high school, even though he was a celebrity

1	⊂A⊃	⊂B⊃	⊂C⊃	⊂D⊃	⊂E⊃
2	⊂A⊃	⊂B⊃	⊂C⊃	⊂D⊃	⊂E⊃
3	⊂A⊃	⊂B⊃	⊂C⊃	⊂D⊃	⊂E⊃
4	⊂A⊃	⊂B⊃	⊂C⊃	⊂D⊃	⊂E⊃
5	⊂A⊃	⊂B⊃	⊂C⊃	⊂D⊃	⊂E⊃
6	⊂A⊃	⊂B⊃	⊂C⊃	⊂D⊃	⊂E⊃

Answers and Explanations: Practice Passage 4

1. **D** This is the first question—which makes it likely that you will find the answer in the first paragraph. Was the book "little-known" as choice A says? No, according to the author it was famous and "an anthem" for the author and his friends. Was the book about high school students, as choice B suggests? No, according to the author it was about a soldier (it was actually during World War II). Was the book too traditional, as choice C suggests? From the description offered in paragraph 2, this was not a traditional book. Traditional books have heroes, not anti-heroes. Inspiring and thoughtful as choice D suggests? Yes, and note that the answer came from the first paragraph. Hold onto this one. Was the book more suited to an older generation as choice E suggests? These kids seemed to like it just fine. The best answer is choice D.

2. **A** You probably had a good idea of the answer to this general question by the time you'd finished your fast read. Was this a profile of Joseph Heller? Of course not. It was mostly about one incident in which the writer of this passage saw and met Heller. Scratch choice B. Choice C might have been tempting but for the word "early" and the "s" on the end of "memories." This passage concerned one memory, and it did not concern the author's early childhood. Choice D reflected a momentary disappointment the author felt, but by the end of the passage he was clearly over it. While the passage does fleetingly describe *Catch-22*, it is mostly devoted to describing the day of Heller's appearance at the school. The best answer is choice A.

3. **D** To answer this EXCEPT question, you have to read a little above the quoted lines, to find out how this sentence fits the context of the entire paragraph. The writer had expected Heller to make the big entrance of a famous person, but instead he just walked up by himself. This tells us something about: choice A, the difference between the writer's picture of Heller and the reality; choice B, the normal way that Heller chose to live his life; choice C, how the writer of the passage was thinking; and choice E, the age of the sneakers themselves. However it does not suggest that Heller had dressed like this just to make an impression on his audience. The best answer is choice D.

4. **D** Choice A is tempting here because clearly by the end of the speech, the wit and imagery of the novelist had captured his audience. However, the purpose of the paragraph was to illustrate the fact that the audience was captured, which makes choice D the best answer. Likewise, choices B and E accurately describe how the students first reacted to Heller, but by the end of the speech, they had changed their minds. Choice C says this paragraph was to respond to charges against Heller's works, but no such charges are made in the passage.

5. **C** The expression, "to field a question" probably has its roots in baseball, where you "field" a hit, but the sense of the word in this case was simply "responded to." There was no reason to suppose that Heller was on the defensive and had to "evade" questions, or that he was so caught up in the questions that he had to "delve" (meaning "go deeper") into them. The best answer is choice C.

6. **B** Get rid of the impossible answer choices. Choice A does not seem like enough of a reason to remember a handshake. Choice D is wrong because the author of the passage ended up being very impressed by Heller. Choice E seems a bit too generic to be the reason the author would remember a handshake from someone he clearly admired a lot. You're down to choices B and C. Was it just because he liked Heller's work, or had he been somehow touched by something deeper? The best answer is choice B.

CRITICAL READING: PRACTICE PASSAGE 5

Each passage below is followed by questions based on its content. Answer the questions on the basis of what is <u>stated</u> or <u>implied</u> in the passage and in any introductory material that may be provided.

Questions 1-9 are based on the following passage.

This passage describes the first detailed observations of the surface of the planet Mars—observations that indirectly led some to the mistaken belief that intelligent life existed there.

The summer of 1877 had been an exceptional time for observing Mars. Every 26 months the slower-moving Mars comes especially close to Earth, creating the most favorable opportunity
Line for observations—or, in the space age, for travel
5 to the planet. Sometimes these opportunities are better than others. Because of the large ellipticy* of the Martian orbit, the distance between Mars and Earth at the closest approach of opposition (when Mars is on the opposite side of Earth from the Sun)
10 varies from as near as 35 million miles to as far as 63 million. The closest of these oppositions occurs approximately every 15 years, and 1877 was one of those choice viewing times.
   Among the astronomers taking advantage of
15 the opportunity was Giovani Virginio Schiaparelli, director of the Milan Observatory and a scientist highly esteemed, particularly for his research concerning meteors and comets. While examining Mars with a relatively small 8-inch telescope,
20 Schiaparelli saw faint linear markings across the disc. Earlier observers had glimpsed some such streaks, but nothing as prominent and widespread as those Schiaparelli described seeing. His drawings of Mars showed the dark areas, which some took to be seas,
25 connected by an extensive network of long straight lines. Schiaparelli called the lines *canali*.
   In Italian, the primary meaning of *canali* is "channels" or "grooves," which is presumably what Schiaparelli intended in the initial announcement of
30 his discovery. He said that they "may be designated as *canali* although we do not yet know what they are." But the word can also mean "canal," which is how it usually was translated. The difference in meanings had tremendous theoretical implications.
35 "The whole hypothesis was right there in the translation," science writer Carl Sagan has said. "Somebody saw canals on Mars. Well, what does that mean? Well, canal—everybody knows what a canal is. How do you get a canal? Somebody builds
40 it. Well, then there are *builders* of canals on Mars."

It may be no coincidence that the Martian canals inspired extravagant speculation at a time when canal building on Earth was a reigning symbol of the Age of Progress. The Suez Canal was
45 completed in 1869, and the first efforts to breach Central America at Nicaragua or Panama were being promoted. To cut through miles of land and join two seas, to mold imperfect nature to suit man—in the nineteenth-century way of thinking, this was surely
50 how intelligent beings met challenges, whether on Earth or on Mars.
   Schiaparelli seemed to be of two minds about the markings. Of the canal-builders' interpretation he once remarked, "I am careful not to combat this
55 suggestion, which contains nothing impossible." But he would not encourage speculation. At another time, Schiaparelli elaborated on observations suggesting to him that the snows and ice of the Martian north pole were associated with the canals.
60 When snows are melting with the change of season, the breadth of the canals increases and temporary seas appear, he noted, and in the winter the canals diminish and some of the seas disappear. But he saw a thoroughly natural explanation for the canals.
65 "It is not necessary to suppose them to be the work of intelligent beings," he wrote in 1893, "and notwithstanding the almost geometrical appearance of all of their system, we are now inclined to believe them to be produced by the evolution of the planet,
70 just as on Earth we have the English Channel."
   His cautionary words had little effect. Those who wanted to believe in a system of water canals on Mars, built by intelligent beings, were not to be discouraged—or proven wrong—for another 70
75 years.

   * *Ellipticy* refers to an oval (rather than a perfectly round) orbit around the sun.

1. Which of the following dates was likely to be the best for viewing Mars?

   (A) 6 months prior to the summer of 1877
   (B) 26 months after the summer of 1877
   (C) 15 years after the summer of 1877
   (D) 26 months before the summer of 1877
   (E) 1 month prior to the summer of 1877

2. In line 13, "choice" most nearly means

   (A) accepted
   (B) optional
   (C) exclusive
   (D) preferred
   (E) selected

3. According to the author, which best indicates the definition of "canali" (line 26) that Schiaparelli most likely originally intended?

   (A) extensive networks
   (B) dark sea-like areas
   (C) channels or grooves
   (D) long canals
   (E) moon-like deserts

4. The author quotes Carl Sagan in lines 35-40, primarily to

   (A) introduce another modern writer's views into his discussion
   (B) illustrate the thought process that led to a misunderstanding
   (C) discuss the feasibility of building canals on Mars
   (D) discount the theories of Schiaparelli
   (E) reveal that the sightings of the *canali* were unsubstantiated and incorrect

5. Which statement best summarizes the point made in the fifth paragraph?

   (A) The sightings of the Mars canals in 1877 led to a surge of canal building on Earth.
   (B) The readiness to believe that the canali were constructed by intelligent beings may have come from a general fascination with canal building at the time.
   (C) The Suez Canal's completion in 1869 set in motion another canal-building project that ultimately became the Panama Canal.
   (D) Canal building is one important way to measure the relative intelligence and development of civilizations.
   (E) Differences in the meaning of the word "canali" caused imperfections in the efforts to join two seas in Central America.

6. The author's tone in using the words, "surely how...on Mars." (lines 49-51) is meant to express

   (A) irony
   (B) despair
   (C) uncertainty
   (D) rage
   (E) apathy

7. In line 52, "of two minds" means

   (A) undecided
   (B) tentative
   (C) changeable
   (D) vague
   (E) skeptical

8. To what did Schiaparelli attribute the periodic changes in the appearance of the Martian canals described in the sixth paragraph?

   (A) The ellipticy of the Martian orbit exerts a tidal pull on the water in the canals.
   (B) The visual distortion of Schiaparelli's relatively small telescope caused the image to change.
   (C) Changes in the distance between Earth and Mars make objects appear to get smaller or larger.
   (D) The canals get inundated by temporary seas.
   (E) Melted ice from the north pole flows into the canals during some seasons, enlarging them.

9. According to the author, what did Schiaparelli ultimately decide about the *canali* he had discovered?

   (A) The *canali* showed that life on Mars is not impossible.
   (B) Their geometrical appearance was misstated: the canals did not exist as straight lines, but as curves.
   (C) They were most likely a phenomena created by nature.
   (D) The canals evolved from less intelligent life.
   (E) They were constructed to provide irrigation to lands far away from the seas.

1 ⊂A⊃ ⊂B⊃ ⊂C⊃ ⊂D⊃ ⊂E⊃
2 ⊂A⊃ ⊂B⊃ ⊂C⊃ ⊂D⊃ ⊂E⊃
3 ⊂A⊃ ⊂B⊃ ⊂C⊃ ⊂D⊃ ⊂E⊃
4 ⊂A⊃ ⊂B⊃ ⊂C⊃ ⊂D⊃ ⊂E⊃
5 ⊂A⊃ ⊂B⊃ ⊂C⊃ ⊂D⊃ ⊂E⊃
6 ⊂A⊃ ⊂B⊃ ⊂C⊃ ⊂D⊃ ⊂E⊃
7 ⊂A⊃ ⊂B⊃ ⊂C⊃ ⊂D⊃ ⊂E⊃
8 ⊂A⊃ ⊂B⊃ ⊂C⊃ ⊂D⊃ ⊂E⊃
9 ⊂A⊃ ⊂B⊃ ⊂C⊃ ⊂D⊃ ⊂E⊃

Answers and Explanations: Practice Passage 5

1. **C** The answer to this first question is, as you might imagine, in the first paragraph. The summer of 1877 had been one of the best times for viewing Mars. According to the passage, every 26 months there was another good opportunity to view Mars, but the best time to observe the planet was every 15 years. Thus, the best answer is in some increment of 15 years before or after the summer of 1877. The best answer is choice C.

2. **D** The "choice viewing time" the author is talking about in the quoted line is one of the occasions referred to in the explanation to question 1, when Earth and Mars are closest and can be most easily viewed with a telescope. In this context, the best definition offered is choice D, "preferred."

3. **C** Re-reading from the beginning of the third paragraph, "...the primary meaning of canali is 'channels' or 'grooves,' which is presumably what Schiaparelli intended..." Well, that's enough for us! The best answer is choice C.

4. **B** Sagan does not discuss whether or not the hypothesis was true, or the feasibility of building canals on Mars, nor does he make fun of Schaparelli, or discredit the sightings of the canali. He merely illustrates how the people at that time reached the conclusion that there might be intelligent life on Mars. The best answer is choice B. Choice A is just kind of odd; would the author mention a modern writer just for the heck of it?

5. **B** Choice A gets the chain of events backward. The Suez canal was finished in 1869—well before the canali were spotted on Mars. The canal across Panama was mentioned in the passage, but it certainly wasn't the main idea of the paragraph—so rule out both choices C and E. It may be that at the time people thought canal-building represented higher intelligence, but once again this was not the main idea of the paragraph, so eliminate choice D.

   The best answer is choice B. Because canal building was trendy at the time on Earth, it made people more interested—and more willing to believe—in the so-called canals on Mars.

6. **A** This part of the passage gently mocks the nineteenth-century people who thought canal building was the highest possible pinnacle of intellectual progress. The best answer is choice A, "irony." If you weren't sure about the correct answer, you could still have eliminated a few choices because they were almost ridiculous. Reading this paragraph, did you think the tone was that of despair, rage, or apathy? These were easy eliminations.

7. **A** In the context of this sentence, Schiaparelli's being "of two minds" did not mean he was changing his mind every five minutes ("changeable"), that he didn't believe in either of the two theories ("skeptical"), that he was indistinct or blurred ("vague"), or that he was feeling experimental ("tentative"). The best answer here is choice A, that he was "undecided."

8. **E** Where did Schiaparelli describe the changes in the canals? That's right: the second to last paragraph. In lines 57–61, he spoke of "observations suggesting to him that the snows and ice of the Martian north pole were associated with the canals. When snows are melting...the breadth of the canals increases." Choice D might have seemed tempting because the temporary seas are mentioned here, but the passage does not say that the seas swallow up the canals. The best answer is choice E.

9. **C** This is the last question, so the answer will probably be found toward the end of the passage. In lines 63–64, the author writes, "But he saw a thoroughly natural explanation for the canals," and then the author quotes Schiaparelli saying, "...we are now inclined to believe [the canals] to be produced by the evolution of the planet...." The best answer is choice C.

CRITICAL READING: PRACTICE PASSAGE 6

Each passage below is followed by questions based on its content. Answer the questions on the basis of what is <u>stated</u> or <u>implied</u> in the passage and in any introductory material that may be provided.

Questions 1-6 are based on the following passage.

In the following excerpt from a novel, Pearl, an elderly woman, is speaking to her son.

Pearl opened her eyes when Ezra turned a page of his magazine. "Ezra," she said. She felt him grow still. He had this habit—he had always had it—of
Line becoming totally motionless when people spoke
5 to him. It was endearing but also in some ways a strain, for then whatever she said to him ("I feel a draft," or "the paper boy is late again") was bound to disappoint him, wasn't it? How could she live up to Ezra's expectations? She plucked at her quilt. "If I
10 could just have some water," she told him.
He poured it from the pitcher on the bureau. She heard no ice cubes clinking; they must have melted. Yet it seemed just minutes ago that he'd brought in a whole new supply. He raised her head, rested
15 it on his shoulder, and tipped the glass to her lips. Yes, lukewarm—not that she minded. She drank gratefully, keeping her eyes closed. His shoulder felt steady and comforting. He laid her back down on the pillow.
20 "Dr. Vincent's coming at ten," he told her.
"What time is it now?"
"Eight-thirty."
"Eight-thirty in the morning?"
"Yes."
25 "Have you been here all night?" she asked.
"I slept a little."
"Sleep now. I won't be needing you."
"Well, maybe after the doctor comes."
It was important to Pearl that she deceive the
30 doctor. She didn't want to go to the hospital. Her illness was pneumonia, she was almost certain; she guessed it from a past experience. She recognized the way it settled into her back. If Dr. Vincent found out he would take her out of her own bed, her own
35 house, and send her off to Union Memorial, tent her over with plastic. "Maybe you should cancel the doctor altogether," she told Ezra. "I'm very much improved, I believe."
"Let him decide that."
40 "Well, I know how my own self feels, Ezra."
"We won't argue about it just now," he said.
He could surprise you, Ezra could. He'd let a

person walk all over him but then display, at odd moments, a deep and rock-hard stubbornness. She
45 sighed and smoothed her quilt. Wasn't it supposed to be the daughter who came and nursed you? She knew she should send him away but she couldn't make herself do it. "I guess you want to get back to that restaurant," she told him.
50 "No, no."
"You're like a mother hen about that place," she said. She sniffed. Then she said, "Ezra, do you smell smoke?"
"Why do you ask?" he said (cautious as ever).
55 "I dreamed the house burned down."
"It didn't really."
"Ah."
She waited, holding herself in. Her muscles were so tense, she ached all over. Finally she said, "Ezra?"
60 "Yes, Mother?"
"Maybe you could just check."
"Check what?"
"The house, of course. Check if it it's on fire."

1. How does the author reveal the passage of time in the second paragraph?

    (A) The sun has just come up.
    (B) The ice cubes in the pitcher have melted.
    (C) Ezra has finally arrived.
    (D) Pearl closes her eyes and dreams.
    (E) The water in the pitcher is cold.

2. It can be inferred from the dialogue in lines 20-28 that Pearl has spent the night

    (A) talking to Ezra about the past
    (B) making plans to go to the hospital
    (C) talking on the telephone to her friends
    (D) sleeping in her bed
    (E) worrying about the future

3. If Ezra knew that Pearl had pneumonia, he would most probably

    (A) agree to let her stay where she is
    (B) insist that she go to the hospital
    (C) make sure that she gets more rest and drinks fluids
    (D) agree to lie to the doctor about her illness in order to help his mother stay out of the hospital
    (E) ask another doctor for a second opinion

4. The passage suggests that in this scene Pearl is

    (A) in the hospital
    (B) staying with Ezra at his house
    (C) living at home
    (D) living in a hotel
    (E) at a health clinic

5. The author writes, " She sighed and smoothed her quilt," (lines 44-45) in order to convey that Pearl

    (A) is exasperated with her son and wishes he would leave her alone
    (B) is tired and wishes to sleep
    (C) has given up trying to persuade Ezra to cancel the doctor
    (D) is a fastidious person who dislikes wrinkled things
    (E) is no longer completely in touch with reality

6. The passage suggests that Pearl's fears that the house is on fire

    (A) are likely to turn out to be true
    (B) have no basis whatsoever
    (C) came as a result of a dream she had
    (D) are just a way to get her son to leave her alone for a moment
    (E) are the result of a sleepless night

	A	B	C	D	E
1	⊂A⊃	⊂B⊃	⊂C⊃	⊂D⊃	⊂E⊃
2	⊂A⊃	⊂B⊃	⊂C⊃	⊂D⊃	⊂E⊃
3	⊂A⊃	⊂B⊃	⊂C⊃	⊂D⊃	⊂E⊃
4	⊂A⊃	⊂B⊃	⊂C⊃	⊂D⊃	⊂E⊃
5	⊂A⊃	⊂B⊃	⊂C⊃	⊂D⊃	⊂E⊃
6	⊂A⊃	⊂B⊃	⊂C⊃	⊂D⊃	⊂E⊃

Answers and Explanations: Practice Passage 6

1 **B** Go back to the second paragraph and read it again. How do you know from this paragraph that time has gone by? Go through the answer choices and do a little elimination. The second paragraph doesn't mention that the sun has come up. Later in the passage, Ezra tells Pearl it is already morning, but he hasn't told her this by the second paragraph. Eliminate choice A. Choice B seems very possible. If Pearl feels that Ezra brought ice only a few minutes ago, and yet the ice has melted, that implies that she has missed some time. Hold on to that one. Choice C is wrong because Ezra has been present all night. Eliminate choice C. Pearl does close her eyes in this passage, but only while she is drinking. It's hard to see the passage of time in a sip of water, so choice D bites the dust. Choice E directly contradicts the passage: the water is not cold—it is now lukewarm. The correct answer must be choice B.

2. **D** At no time in this passage is the answer to this question stated directly. However there are a series of clues. First, Pearl opens her eyes at the beginning. Second, the ice cubes that Ezra had brought "it seemed just minutes ago" were already melted. And third, she doesn't know whether it is day or night. What has she been doing? That's right: getting some z's. The best answer is choice D.

3. **B** This question has no line number, but it's easy to find the lead word "pneumonia" in line 31.

   If Ezra knew Pearl had pneumonia, what would he do about it? This is a hypothetical question. To answer it, you must think about what you know of Ezra. He stayed with Pearl all night. When she drank some water, he propped her up with his own shoulder. And he refused to go to sleep until after he'd heard what the doctor had to say. Given all this, what do you think he would do if he knew she had pneumonia? The best answer is choice B.

4. **C** Again, there is no line number, but the answer to question 4 is likely to come right after the answer to question 3.

   When you first started the passage, you may have leapt to the conclusion that she was in the hospital already. However, there is one key place in the passage where you find out exactly where she is: lines 33–36. Here, directly stated, is her intention to try to avoid going to the hospital (meaning she isn't there now) and her intention to stay in "her own bed, her own house." The only possible answer is choice C.

5. **C** As always, you should read a little bit above and below the cited line to understand the context of the quoted words. Pearl has been trying to persuade Ezra not to let the doctor come, but he has been stubborn and without actually saying no, has indicated he will not cancel the doctor's visit. Choices B, D, and E do not seem to have anything to do with what has just happened. Both choices A and C could be legitimate reactions to Ezra's refusal to let her have her way. But "sighing" seems more a sign of resignation than of anger. The best answer is choice C.

6. **C** There is no real indication that the house is actually on fire, so eliminate choice A, but Pearl's fears are not based on nothing—she has had a dream. Thus, eliminate choice B, and the best answer is choice C. Choice D is theoretically possible, but not supported by the text. Choice E is contradicted by the fact that Pearl has been dreaming.

CRITICAL READING: PRACTICE PASSAGE 7

Each passage below is followed by questions based on its content. Answer the questions on the basis of what is <u>stated</u> or <u>implied</u> in the passage and in any introductory material that may be provided.

Questions 1-12 are based on the following passage.

The following two passages present two views of the funeral industry in the United States. The first passage is an excerpt from a book written in 1963 by a journalist and takes a hard look at funeral practices at the time. The second passage was written in the 1980s by a member of the funeral business and looks at the changes in the industry since the first book appeared.

Passage 1

Oh death, where is thy sting? O grave, where is thy victory? Where, indeed. Many a badly stung survivor faced with the aftermath of some relative's
Line funeral has ruefully concluded that the victory has
5 been won hands down by a funeral establishment—
in disastrously unequal battle.

Much has been written of late about the affluent society in which we live, and much fun poked at some of the irrational "status symbols" set out
10 like golden snares to trap the unwary consumer at every turn. Until recently, little has been said about the most irrational and weirdest of the lot, lying in ambush for all of us at the end of the road—the modern American funeral.
15 If the dismal traders (as an eighteenth-century English writer calls them) have traditionally been cast in a comic role in literature, a universally recognized symbol of humor from Shakespeare to Dickens to Evelyn Waugh, they have successfully
20 turned the tables in recent years to perpetrate a huge, macabre, and expensive practical joke on the American public. It is not consciously conceived of as a joke, of course; on the contrary, it is hedged with admirably contrived rationalizations.
25 Gradually, almost imperceptibly, over the years, the funeral men have constructed their own grotesque cloud-cuckoo-land where the trappings of Gracious Living are transformed, as in a nightmare, into the trappings of Gracious Dying. The same
30 familiar Madison Avenue language has seeped into the funeral industry.

So that this too, too solid flesh might not melt, we are offered "solid copper—a quality casket which offers superb value to the client seeking long-lasting
35 protection," or the "colonial Classic Beauty—18 gauge lead-coated steel, seamless top, lap-jointed welded body construction." Some caskets are equipped with foam rubber, some with innerspring mattresses. One company actually offers "the
40 revolutionary Perfect-Posture bed."

Passage 2

In the past 20 years, many of the questionable excesses of the funeral trade have been curbed: legislation and self-policing by funeral home associations have brought some measure of
45 regulation to an industry that was at one time sadly deficient. And yet, if the sharp practices of shoddy morticians are no longer cause for customers to "whirl in their urns," as Jessica Mitford once put it so trenchantly, I fear that we may have somehow
50 tilted too far in the other direction.

True, the costs of funerals in the 1960s were escalating out of all proportion to real value, but I am convinced that in our search for economy and avoidance of discomfort we have weakened
55 a very important family rite. Consider the case of one funeral "park" in Southern California that has instituted "drive-in" funerals. Believe it or not, you can view the remains, attend the chapel service, and witness the interment—all without leaving your car.
60 To the extent that measures such as these have cut costs, I would applaud, but in my opinion these measures have also produced a disconnection from the real purposes of a funeral. The process of spending time mourning the dead fills a real need
65 for the bereaved. There is a purpose to each of the steps of a funeral, and if there is a commensurate cost to those steps, then so be it. These days it is possible to have a funeral without a service for friends and family to gather, without a graveside
70 interment, even without a casket. More frequently now, families will ask that contributions to charity be made in lieu of flowers and wreaths—without recognizing that buying flowers provides a chance for friends and relatives to show their concern in a
75 more tangible way than a gift to charity.

Let us not forget that feelings are as important as economy.

1. Why does the author of the first passage use the quote "O, death, where is thy sting?" (line 1)

   (A) To introduce the subject of death in a literary fashion
   (B) As a quick way to get people's attention
   (C) To suggest that the sting of death can also affect the living who must pay for the funeral
   (D) To illustrate that funeral directors are caring members of a sensitive profession
   (E) To suggest that death has no affect on the author of this passage

2. According to the passage, the "dismal traders" mentioned in line 15 are

   (A) undertakers
   (B) shopkeepers
   (C) writers such as Shakespeare and Dickens
   (D) practical jokers
   (E) stock and bond salesmen

3. According to the fourth and fifth paragraphs of the first passage, to sell their new products, funeral directors are using

   (A) free consultation and advice sessions
   (B) incentive plans designed to get customers to purchase funerals while they are still alive
   (C) the language of advertising
   (D) family specials
   (E) young spokespersons who are skilled at sales tactics

4. The tone of the first passage's author could best be described as

   (A) nostalgic
   (B) ironic
   (C) happy
   (D) indifferent
   (E) lyrical

5. If the author of the first passage were to plan her funeral in advance, which of the following would she most likely try to do?

   (A) Buy an expensive casket with a Perfect Posture mattress inside
   (B) Invite her friends to a service at a funeral home
   (C) Buy a burial plot overlooking a river
   (D) Prepay her funeral so that it could be as elaborate as possible
   (E) Leave instructions for a simple, inexpensive funeral

6. In line 42, "curbed" most nearly means

   (A) brought under control
   (B) kept under wraps
   (C) led aside
   (D) established
   (E) kept at a constant level

7. According to the second passage, the excesses of the funeral trade have been changed for the better as a result of

   (A) the passage of time
   (B) the institution of services such as drive-in funerals
   (C) the elimination of flowers and wreaths at services
   (D) new government laws and trade association rules
   (E) the practices of shoddy morticians

8. The author cites the example of the "drive-in funerals" (line 57) in order to

   (A) illustrate the point that such practices take away from the real purposes of a funeral
   (B) condemn the people who consent to mourn in this way
   (C) demonstrate the ways in which the funeral industry has changed for the better
   (D) respond to charges that the industry is still sadly deficient
   (E) rebut claims that the industry has failed to change in the past twenty years

9. The phrase "in lieu of" (line 72) most nearly means

  (A) as well as
  (B) because of
  (C) instead of
  (D) in addition to
  (E) on the side of

10. The contrast between the two descriptions of the funeral industry is essentially one between

  (A) rank pessimism and new-found dread
  (B) greedy opportunism and mature professionalism
  (C) uncertain pride and unsure self-esteem
  (D) jealous warnings and alert alarms
  (E) lawless exhaustion and tireless energy

11. Both authors indicate that the funeral industry

  (A) continues to engage in shoddy practices
  (B) fulfills a real need in the community
  (C) can police itself
  (D) preys on the suffering of the bereaved
  (E) was in a troubled state in the 1960s

12. The contrast between the two passages reflects primarily the biases of

  (A) an older woman and a younger man
  (B) a native of the United States and a native of Europe
  (C) an optimist and a pessimist
  (D) an investigative journalist and a member of the funeral industry
  (E) a person from the east coast, and a person from the west coast

1 ⊂A⊃ ⊂B⊃ ⊂C⊃ ⊂D⊃ ⊂E⊃
2 ⊂A⊃ ⊂B⊃ ⊂C⊃ ⊂D⊃ ⊂E⊃
3 ⊂A⊃ ⊂B⊃ ⊂C⊃ ⊂D⊃ ⊂E⊃
4 ⊂A⊃ ⊂B⊃ ⊂C⊃ ⊂D⊃ ⊂E⊃
5 ⊂A⊃ ⊂B⊃ ⊂C⊃ ⊂D⊃ ⊂E⊃
6 ⊂A⊃ ⊂B⊃ ⊂C⊃ ⊂D⊃ ⊂E⊃
7 ⊂A⊃ ⊂B⊃ ⊂C⊃ ⊂D⊃ ⊂E⊃
8 ⊂A⊃ ⊂B⊃ ⊂C⊃ ⊂D⊃ ⊂E⊃
9 ⊂A⊃ ⊂B⊃ ⊂C⊃ ⊂D⊃ ⊂E⊃
10 ⊂A⊃ ⊂B⊃ ⊂C⊃ ⊂D⊃ ⊂E⊃
11 ⊂A⊃ ⊂B⊃ ⊂C⊃ ⊂D⊃ ⊂E⊃
12 ⊂A⊃ ⊂B⊃ ⊂C⊃ ⊂D⊃ ⊂E⊃

Answers and Explanations: Practice Passage 7

1. **C** Reading just a little further past the cited line, it becomes clear that the author thinks that one of death's stings these days is the bill relatives have to pay for the funeral. While you could make an argument for both choices A and B, choice C is the best answer.

2. **A** This question is a bit difficult. The author does not spell out her meaning here, but the entire passage is about the funeral industry, so it is a logical inference that the "dismal traders" are, in fact, undertakers. While Dickens and Shakespeare are mentioned in the paragraph, it is fairly clear from the context that they are not the "dismal traders." Similarly, while the passage says the dismal traders have perpetrated a practical joke, it also says that this joke is not "consciously conceived of as a joke," and thus it seems incorrect to call them practical jokers. The best answer is choice A.

3. **C** It is in the fourth and fifth paragraphs that the author talks about new funeral products. In those paragraphs she says that the funeral industry uses the vocabulary of "Madison Avenue"—a common reference to the advertising industry. She also quotes the industry's jargon to describe its products, and the jargon sounds just like the phrases you would read in an advertisement for a new car.

4. **B** The author is certainly making fun of the funeral industry, mocking its language and its practices. Her tone is not nostalgic, happy, indifferent, or lyrical. It is ironic, choice B.

5. **E** After reading the passage it is clear that the author detests expensive, overblown funerals. The best answer is choice E.

6. **A** The key to this vocabulary question came in the same sentence as the key to question 6: "The excesses...have been curbed" by legislation, etc., that "have brought some measure of regulation...to the industry." Effectively, "curbed" means to bring excesses under regulation. Which answer choices are close to this meaning? The only two possibilities are choices A and E. Now, does the author mean that the "questionable excesses" of the funeral industry have been brought under control or kept at a constant level? Because it's clear she believes the situation has improved, the best answer choice is A.

7. **D** The answer to this question can be found in the first paragraph of the second passage, right after the colon in the first sentence: "...legislation and self-policing by funeral home associations have brought some measure of regulation...." Thus the best answer is choice D. Choices B and C, while economies that might help customers, are not broad enough to stop the excesses of an entire industry.

8. **A** The example of the "drive-in" is introduced with the words "Consider the case of..." Obviously this is meant to be an example to illustrate a point that was just made: "...that in our search for economy and avoidance of discomfort, we have weakened a very important family rite." Which answer choice resembles this sentiment? If you said choice A, you were right. Choice B is tempting because the author does seem to be condemning drive-in funerals, but the point of the example is not to make fun of the people who attend, but to point out an important feature that these funerals lack.

9. **C** If you weren't sure what "in lieu of" meant, the second half of the sentence might help. Here, the author makes it clear that if a contribution has been made "in lieu of" flowers, then the contributors have not bought the flowers. Get rid of choices A, D, and E. Substituting "because of" for "in lieu of" does not produce an understandable sentence. Hence, the best answer is choice C.

10. **B** The first passage paints a bleak view of an industry run amok— overcharging customers left and right. The second passage portrays a more mature, self-policing industry. The best answer is choice B. Because you know from the introductory material that the two passages are presenting at least slightly differing opinions on the same subject, it is easy to eliminate choices A and C, which do not offer contrasting visions of the industry.

11. **E** The second passage maintains that the funeral industry is much better than it used to be, so eliminate choices A and D. The first passage would disagree with choices B and C, allowing us to eliminate them as well.

   The introductory material was crucial to understanding the answer to this question. The first passage was written during the 1960s and detailed the harmful practices of the funeral trade. The second passage was written during the 1980s and looked back 20 years to the same harmful practices. The best answer is choice E.

12. **D** The answer to this question is also found in the introductory material. The ages, nationalities, and regions of the two writers were not discussed, so eliminate choices A, B, and E. While you may have felt the first passage was written by a pessimist and the second by an optimist, choice D is slightly better than choice C.

   On the following pages, you will find a practice Reading Comprehension section, similar to what you will find on the SAT. Give yourself exactly 25 minutes to complete this test section. Good luck!

SECTION 2
Time — 25 minutes
24 Questions

Turn to Section 2 of your answer sheet to answer the questions in this section.

Directions: For each question in this section, select the best answer from among the choices given and fill in the corresponding circle on the answer sheet.

Each sentence below has one or two blanks, each blank indicating that something has been omitted. Beneath the sentence are five words or sets of words labeled A through E. Choose the word or set of words that, when inserted in the sentence, best fits the meaning of the sentence as a whole.

Example:

Hoping to ------- the dispute, negotiators proposed a compromise that they felt would be ------- to both labor and management.

(A) enforce . . useful
(B) end . . divisive
(C) overcome . . unattractive
(D) extend . . satisfactory
(E) resolve . . acceptable

Ⓐ Ⓑ Ⓒ Ⓓ ●

---

1. The work of Max Weber, an early social theorist, was ------- by a student who aided in collecting and organizing a plethora of data.

   (A) prevented   (B) compromised   (C) limited
       (D) facilitated   (E) created

2. However ------- were Marvin Gaye's beginnings as a member of his father's church choir, he became a famous and ------- performer.

   (A) powerful . . wealthy
   (B) popular . . unqualified
   (C) inspiring . . notorious
   (D) humble . . spiritual
   (E) modest . . esteemed

3. Sustainable development is characterized by political -------, with conservationists, oil companies, and public officials each advocating different solutions.

   (A) approval   (B) shrewdness   (C) distinction
       (D) discord   (E) upheaval

4. Although destructive wildfires are often thought to be -------, they are sometimes actually -------, allowing for the growth of new plant and animal species.

   (A) dangerous . . peripheral
   (B) deleterious . . beneficial
   (C) despoiled . . advantageous
   (D) wretched . . exultant
   (E) ruinous . . archaic

5. A painter's ability to render a likeness is both ------- and acquired; the artist blends natural abilities with worldly experience in the creation of his or her art.

   (A) anticipated   (B) overt   (C) aesthetic
       (D) ubiquitous   (E) innate

6. Unlike its counterpart in Manhattan, Brooklyn's Broadway is ------- by an elevated train track that blocks out the sun and casts a gloomy shadow over the street.

   (A) shrouded   (B) substantiated   (C) perpetuated
       (D) articulated   (E) supplanted

7. The interviewer is known for ------- his guests by asking them overly personal questions.

   (A) chronicling   (B) disconcerting
       (C) upbraiding   (D) mocking   (E) distracting

8. Even though their parents were convinced that they were ------- children, the boys were often in trouble at school and on the playground for ------- behavior.

   (A) reprehensible . . pugnacious
   (B) innovative . . compelling
   (C) exemplary . . fractious
   (D) prodigious . . fastidious
   (E) listless . . indolent

GO ON TO THE NEXT PAGE

Each passage below is followed by questions based on its content. Answer the questions on the basis of what is <u>stated</u> or <u>implied</u> in each passage and in any introductory material that may be provided.

Questions 9-10 are based on the following passage.

Since 1970, national parks have had to double the number of signs warning visitors of possible hazards. The new signs have a dual purpose in
Line that they also protect the parks from unnecessary
5 litigation. In 1972, the National Parks Service in Yellowstone was forced to pay more than $87,000 to the victim of a bear attack. This ruling prompted Yellowstone historian Lee Whittlesley to write, "Analogously I could ask, should New York's
10 Central Park have signs every ten feet saying, 'Danger! Muggers!' just because a non-streetwise, non-New Yorker might go walking there?"

9.   Which of the following can be inferred from the passage above?

(A) Before the judge's ruling, Yellowstone contained no signs warning of bear attacks.
(B) The only purpose of the new signs is to protect the National Parks Service from possible lawsuits.
(C) The National Parks Service can be held responsible for the safety of its visitors.
(D) The National Parks Service is more concerned with lawsuits than the well-being of endangered animals.
(E) Visitors to New York's Central Park have the right to sue the city in the event of a mugging.

10.   The author's attitude toward the National Parks Service in this passage could best be described as

(A) professional disinterest
(B) detached curiosity
(C) mild worry
(D) bitter scorn
(E) measured sympathy

Questions 11-12 are based on the following passage.

Franz Kafka's stories are so abstruse and his literary style so unique that a word, "Kafkaesque," was coined to describe situations that are at once
Line bizarre, illogical, and unfathomable. Kafka's
5 "The Metamorphosis," for example, has spawned hundreds of possible interpretations, ranging from Freudian psychoanalytical discussions of the characters' histories to Marxist readings that focus on the alienation of the worker from society. At
10 least one literary critic specifically attributes Kafka's unique style to the stilted relationship between Kafka and his father, Hermann.

11.   The author's attitude toward Kafka's literary achievements is best described as one of

(A) frustration at the inscrutableness of Kafka's work
(B) recognition for the individuality of Kafka's work
(C) indifference toward the range of possible interpretations of Kafka's work
(D) unabashed appreciation for Kafka's contributions to literature
(E) disappointment at the lack of meaning found in Kafka's fiction

12.   Which of the following can be inferred from the passage?

(A) The work of Franz Kafka, even though it is mostly inscrutable, will continue to mystify and delight readers.
(B) An author's personal history may be relevant to an analysis of his writing.
(C) Freudian psychoanalytical interpretations, along with Marxist readings, are particularly useful approaches to understanding Kafka's works.
(D) Franz Kafka's fiction is so abstruse and so resistant to interpretation that a new word, "Kafkaesque," had to be coined to describe it.
(E) "The Metamorphosis" is Kafka's greatest literary achievement.

GO ON TO THE NEXT PAGE ⟶

Questions 13-24 are based on the following passage.

The following passage relates some conclusions the author draws after listening to a seminar speaker denounce some modern conveniences for their negative effects on people's personal lives.

Several weeks ago, when the weather was still
fine, I decided to eat my lunch on the upper quad,
an expanse of lawn stretching across the north end
5 of campus and hedged in by ancient pine trees on
one side and university buildings on the other.
Depositing my brown paper lunch bag on the grass
beside me, I munched in silence, watching the trees
ripple in the wind and musing over the latest in a
10 series of "controversial" symposiums I had attended
that morning. The speaker, an antiquated professor
in suspenders and a mismatched cardigan, had
delivered an earnest diatribe against modern tools
of convenience like electronic mail and instant
15 messaging programs. I thought his speech was
interesting, but altogether too romantic.

My solitude was broken by two girls, deep in
conversation, who approached from behind and sat
down on the grass about ten feet to my left. I stared
20 hard at my peanut butter sandwich, trying to not
eavesdrop, but their stream of chatter intrigued me.
They interrupted each other frequently, paused at
the same awkward moments, and responded to each
other's statements as if neither one heard what the
25 other said. Confused, I stole a glance at them out
of the corner of my eye. I could tell that they were
college students by their style of dress and the heavy
backpacks sinking into the grass beside them. Their
body language and proximity also indicated that
30 they were friends. Instead of talking to each other,
however, each one was having a separate dialogue
on her cell phone.

As I considered this peculiar scene, this
morning's bleary-eyed lecturer again intruded into
35 my thoughts. His point in the symposium was that,
aside from the disastrous effects of emails and
chatting on the spelling, grammar, and punctuation
of the English language, these modern conveniences
also considerably affect our personal lives. Before
40 the advent of electronic mail, people wrote letters.
Although writing out words by hand posed an
inconvenience, it also conferred certain important
advantages. The writer had time to think about
his message, about how he could best phrase it in
45 order to help his reader understand him, about

how he could convey his emotions without the use
of dancing and flashing smiley face icons. When
he finished his letter, he had created a permanent
work of art to which a hurriedly typed email or
50 abbreviated chat room conversation could never
compare. The temporary, impersonal nature of
computers, Professor Spectacles concluded, is
gradually rendering our lives equally temporary
and impersonal.

55 And what about cell phones? I thought. I have
attended classes where students, instead of turning
off their cell phones for the duration of the lecture,
leave the classroom to take calls without the
slightest hint of embarrassment. I have sat in movie
60 theaters and ground my teeth in frustration at the
person behind me who can't wait until the movie is
over to give his colleague a scene-by-scene replay.
And then I watched each girl next to me spend her
lunch hour talking to someone else instead of her
65 friend. Like the rest of the world, these two pay a
significant price for the benefits of convenience and
the added safety of being in constant contact with
the world. When they have a cell phone, they are
never alone, but then again, *they are never alone.*

70 They may not recognize it, but those girls, like
most of us, could use a moment of solitude. Cell
phones make it so easy to reach out and touch
someone that they have us confused into thinking
that being alone is the same thing as being lonely.
75 It's all right to disconnect from the world every once
in a while; in fact, I feel certain that our sanity and
identity as humans necessitates it. And I'm starting
to think that maybe the Whimsical Professor ranting
about his "technological opiates" is not so romantic
80 after all.

13. As used in the first paragraph, the word "dia-
    tribe" (line 13) most nearly means

    (A) excessive praise
    (B) vengeful speech
    (C) sincere congratulations
    (D) harsh criticism
    (E) factual explanation

GO ON TO THE NEXT PAGE

14. The author's reference to "smiley face icons" (line 47) suggests

(A) a desire to return to a time before electronic mail
(B) skepticism that technology is an unequivocal boon
(C) chagrin at the callousness of modern writers
(D) a longing to create a permanent work of art
(E) relief that most modern writers avoid verbosity

15. Which of the following examples, if true, would strengthen the symposium speaker's argument as described in the third paragraph?

(A) A newlywed couple sends copies of a generic thank-you card from an Internet site to wedding guests.
(B) A high school student uses a graphing program for her algebra homework.
(C) A former high school class president uses the Internet to locate and invite all members of the class to a reunion.
(D) A publisher utilizes an editing program to proofread texts before printing.
(E) A hostess uses her computer to design and print nameplates for all her party guests.

16. The author mentions all of the following examples of the negative effects of modern technology EXCEPT

(A) a student leaves class to take a cell phone call
(B) two friends spend their lunch hour talking on their respective cell phones
(C) a cell phone user disturbs other patrons at a movie theater
(D) email writers compose and send messages without regard to spelling and grammar
(E) a professor delivers a polemic against "technological opiates"

17. As used in lines 16 and 79, the word "romantic" most nearly means

(A) charming and debonair
(B) given to expressions of love
(C) a follower of Romanticism
(D) demonstrating absurd behavior
(E) imaginative but impractical

18. The main idea of the passage is that

(A) modern forms of communication encourage users to disregard conventions of written English
(B) the instruments of modern technology may have a negative impact on our personal and social lives
(C) computers and cell phones destroy the romantic aspect of relationships
(D) the devices used by modern societies to communicate are temporary and impersonal
(E) one teacher's opinion about a controversial subject does not constitute fact

19. According to the passage, writing out words by hand

  I. offers time to think about how best to express ideas and feelings
  II. allows people to grow closer
  III. can be tiresome

(A) I only
(B) III only
(C) I and II only
(D) I and III only
(E) II and III only

20. The purpose of the third paragraph is to

(A) contradict the symposium speaker's argument
(B) continue the story begun in the previous paragraph
(C) elucidate the mystery of the girls' conversations
(D) justify the author's belief that cell phones are physically harmful
(E) explain the main points of the symposium speaker's address

GO ON TO THE NEXT PAGE

21. The speaker at the symposium was most likely in the field of
    (A) psychology
    (B) art history
    (C) literature
    (D) computer science
    (E) mass media

22. In line 69, the author italicizes "they are never alone" primarily to
    (A) emphasize the importance of the phrase
    (B) indicate that the phrase is a translation
    (C) suggest that the phrase is metaphoric
    (D) imply an alternate meaning of the phrase
    (E) denote that the expression is colloquial

23. Which of the following would be the best title for a speech countering the arguments of the "Whimsical Professor" (line 78) ?
    (A) "The Romance of Written Communication"
    (B) "Too Convenient?: Benefits and Costs of Instant Communication"
    (C) "Undoing the Damage of Technological Opiates"
    (D) "Spelling Reform for the Computer Age"
    (E) "Ties That Bind: How Electronic Communication Brings Us Together"

24. The author's attitude toward the symposium speaker can best be described as
    (A) assent tinged with irreverence
    (B) agreement strengthened by admiration
    (C) doubt mixed with scorn
    (D) disbelief bolstered by dislike
    (E) adoration touched by romance

STOP

If you finish before time is called, you may check your work on this section only.
Do not turn to any other section in the test.

NO TEST MATERIAL ON THIS PAGE.

PRACTICE SECTION:
ANSWERS AND EXPLANATIONS

1. **D** Choice D is correct because the clue in the sentence is *aided*. A good phrase to use for the blank is "helped out." None of the other answer choices agrees with the clue.

2. **E** Start with the second blank. You know that Marvin Gaye is *famous*, so the blank is going to mean something close to *famous*. Eliminate Choice B and Choice D. Choice C should also be eliminated because *notorious* means "famous for a bad reason," which is not indicated in the sentence. For the first blank, the word *however* tells you to choose something that is the opposite of famous. *Powerful* is not the opposite of famous, so eliminate Choice A and choose Choice E.

3. **D** The clue in this sentence is *each advocating different solutions*. This suggests that the blank may mean "disagreement." Choice D means disagreement. Choice E is a sudden, violent disruption, which is too extreme. Choice C is not quite strong enough to indicate disagreement. Choice A and Choice B do not agree with the clue.

4. **B** The sentence tells you that wildfires are *destructive*; therefore, you are looking for a similar word to fill the first blank. The second blank must be the opposite of the first because of the words *although* and *actually;* a good word for the second blank would be "helpful." Choice B is therefore correct because it comes closest to the right meaning for both blanks. None of the other answer choices agrees with the clues.

5. **E** The clue for the blank is *the artist blends natural abilities with worldly experience*. A good word to use for the blank would be "inborn." Choice E means just that. None of the other answer choices agrees with the clue.

6. **A** The clue is *blocks out the sun*. A good word for the blank would be "hidden"; Choice A is closest to this meaning. This would also eliminate Choice B, Choice C, and Choice D. Choice E means "to replace, especially by force," and that is not what is needed here.

7. **B** Choice B is correct because the clue *asking them overly personal questions* indicates that the interviewer may make the guests feel uneasy, which is what something *disconcerting* does. None of the other answer choices agrees with the clue.

8. **C** Choice C is correct because the phrase *in trouble* indicates some type of bad behavior for the second blank. This would eliminate Choice B and Choice D. The parents believe the opposite based on the phrase *even though,* so the first word should describe good behavior. This would eliminate Choice A and Choice E.

9. **C** Choice C is correct because the passage says the judge ruled that the parks had too few warning signs in the case of a bear attack. You don't know that there were no warnings, as Choice A implies, and Choice D doesn't really make sense, considering how politically correct the test is. Choice B is not indicated in the passage and uses extreme language. Choice E is incorrect because the passage draws the analogy of *New York's Central Park* to point out the lack of common sense in the judge's ruling.

10. **E** Choice E is correct because *unnecessary litigation* is a clue that the author sympathizes with the National Parks Service's legal difficulties. Because of the author's sympathy, Choice B is incorrect. The author is definitely not disinterested (Choice A), worried (Choice C), or scornful (Choice D) toward the National Parks Service.

11. **B** Choice B is correct because the author twice refers to the *unique* nature of Kafka's work. Choice A is incorrect because the author does not feel Kafka's work is frustrating. Choice C is incorrect because the author refers to *hundreds of possible interpretations*. Choice D and Choice E are not supported in the passage.

12. **B** Choice B is correct because it is the only choice that encompasses the entire passage. Choice A is too specific and tells the future; you don't know that Kafka's work will *continue to mystify*. Choice C is not supported; the author does not discuss the usefulness of these approaches. Choice D contradicts the passage; *Kafkaesque* describes odd, real-life situations, not Kafka's works. Choice E is not mentioned in the passage.

13. **D** The word *against* indicates that the professor's speech is negative. This context eliminates Choice A and Choice C. Choice E and Choice B are not indicated in the passage. Choice D correctly defines *diatribe* as it is used in the context of the passage.

14. **B** The line in question argues that the unavailability of *dancing and flashing smiley face icons* meant that a writer had to think *about how he could convey his emotions* and that being forced to think about this issue was one of the *important advantages* of writing letters by hand (lines 41–51). The development of smiley face icons, therefore, was not entirely a good thing; to use the language in Choice B, the author is indeed skeptical that this particular piece of technology is an unequivocal boon. We can also eliminate Choice E on this basis because the author is arguing that writing letters by hand isn't all bad. However, the author does admit that it isn't all good, either—*writing out words by hand posed an inconvenience* (lines 41–42)—and so you cannot assume that the author wants to return to the past as stated in Choice A. Choice C is too extreme, as the looser standards of modern writers don't mean they are actually unfeeling or callous, and while the author does say that a letter-writer of the past *had created a permanent work of art* (lines 48–49), there's no evidence that the author is longing to do so as stated in Choice D.

15. **A**   Choice A is an example of a couple whose use of technology makes their messages more impersonal than handwritten thank-you cards. None of the other answer choices indicates examples of society being made less personal by technology.

16. **E**   Choice A is mentioned in lines 55–59. Choice B is the subject of the second paragraph and is discussed again in lines 63–65. Choice C appears in lines 59–62. Choice D is strongly hinted at in lines 31–42. But while Choice E is an event related in the passage, it is not a direct effect of modern technology, nor does the author consider it negative: The author calls the speech *interesting* (line 13) and spends much of the passage contemplating it. Therefore, Choice E is the correct answer.

17. **E**   Choice A, Choice C, and Choice D are not indicated in the passage. Choice B is one definition of *romantic,* but the passage does not support the definition of *romantic* as love. Choice E is correct because the author indicates that the professor is *antiquated* (which means old or outdated), suggesting his idea is impractical.

18. **B**   Choice B correctly states the main idea of the passage without being too specific. Choice A is outside the scope of the passage. Choice C, Choice D, and Choice E do not reflect the passage's central subject.

19. **D**   Choice D is the best answer. The passage states that *writing out words by hand posed an inconvenience,* as in III. Therefore, you can eliminate Choice A and Choice C. However, it also gave the writer *time to think about his message and how he could convey his emotions,* as in I. Therefore, you can eliminate Choice B and Choice E. The passage discusses how one can best express oneself through communication, but does not say that that writing by hand *allows people to grow closer* to others, as in II.

20. **E**   The third paragraph relates the details of the symposium speaker's idea, as the author remembers them. Choice A is not supported because the author does not contradict the speaker. The paragraph interrupts the story begun previously; therefore, eliminate Choice B. The mystery of the girls' conversation is solved in the last sentence of the second paragraph, so eliminate Choice C. The passage does not indicate that the author believes cell phones are physically harmful; therefore, Choice D is not supported.

21. **C**   Choice C is the best answer: The symposium speaker is most concerned with issues such as *spelling, grammar, and punctuation of the English language* and how writers could *best phrase* their words to create a *permanent work of art,* all interests of an English professor. Although aspects of Choice B, Choice D, and Choice E are discussed in his speech, they are not the primary emphasis, nor does the speaker show expertise or enjoyment in them. There is nothing in the passage to support Choice A.

22. **D** Choice D suggests that the author repeats and italicizes the phrase to help the reader reconsider its meaning. *They are never alone* can mean that they never have to feel lonely, but also that they can never get a moment to themselves if they want some solitude. Choice A is close, but too general. Choice B is not supported, as there is nothing in the passage to suggest that the phrase is a translation. Choice C is not supported, as there is no use of metaphor here. The phrase is not more informal than the rest of the passage; therefore, eliminate Choice E.

23. **E** The main point the *Whimsical Professor* (line 78) makes, as described in lines 51–54, is that communication by computer makes people's relationships *temporary and impersonal*. A speech that counters the professor's, therefore, would argue that electronic communication does the opposite: it forges strong relationships. Choice E is a good summary of such a speech. Choice A sounds more like it would be on the same side as the professor, praising and even arguing for a return to written communication. Choice B is a good summary of the author's even-handed approach but does not answer the question. Choice C suggests that the professor is right in his assessment that electronic communication is damaging. Choice D doesn't address the professor's main point, and it is hard to tell whether the speaker would agree or disagree with the professor's views about spelling in any case. Choice E is therefore the best answer.

24. **A** The author ends up agreeing with most of the speaker's views, but emphasizes his *whimsical* attributes and *mismatched clothing* and refers to him as *Professor Spectacles*, making Choice A the best answer. Choice B and Choice E are too wholeheartedly positive, while Choice C and Choice D are far more negative than the passage warrants.

5

Grammar

GRAMMAR

Quick—identify the correlative conjunction in the nonrestrictive clause in the following sentence:

> **1.** Just kidding!

Fortunately, the grammar tested on the SAT is not going to be that difficult. Rather, the grammar and writing skills section requires you to know only a few basic rules. ETS will test these rules with three types of questions: error identification, improving sentences, and improving paragraphs.

ERROR IDENTIFICATION QUESTIONS

Error identification questions on the SAT look like this:

> **1.** <u>Most people</u> believe that it is silly <u>to attempt to</u>
>   A   B
>
> test <u>one's</u> writing skills <u>in</u> a multiple-choice
>   C   B
>
> format. <u>No error</u>
>   E

Your task is to figure out which part of the sentence is incorrect. Note that about 20 percent of the error identification questions have no error (if you're curious, this sentence is fine as written).

IMPROVING SENTENCES QUESTIONS

A total of 25 questions in the two grammar sections will be of the improving sentences variety. Improving questions make up the first 11 questions in the 25-minute Writing section and all 14 of those in the 10-minute section. These questions require you to not only to identify an error, but also to fix it.

> **2.** The Macaroni Penguin, along with the Erect-Crested, Fjordland, Rockhopper, Royal, and Snare Island Penguins, <u>have a crest of yellow feathers on their heads</u>.
>
> (A) have a crest of yellow feathers on their heads
> (B) has a crest of yellow feathers on its head
> (C) having crests of yellow feathers on their heads
> (D) all have a crest of yellow feathers on its head
> (E) each with a crest of yellow feathers on its head

Choice A is always a reproduction of the underlined portion of the sentence as written; again, about one-fifth of improving sentences are correct as written. Unfortunately, this sentence is not. The correct answer here is choice B. Not sure why? Read on.

THE PRINCETON REVIEW METHOD

Step One Familiarize yourself with the most commonly tested grammatical errors. ETS tests only a handful of errors. Once you learn these rules and become comfortable with them, keep your eyes peeled for them on the test.

Step Two Make aggressive use of the Process of Elimination. If you're not sure what the right answer is, find and eliminate any answers you know to be wrong. Learn what ETS considers "good" writing.

COMMON GRAMMATICAL ERRORS

PRONOUN ERRORS

Pronouns are one of ETS's favorite grammar subjects to test. When you see a pronoun underlined, check to see if it agrees with the noun it replaces and is in the proper case. Remember: The following pronouns are singular:

anybody	everybody	somebody	nobody	anyone	everyone	someone	no one
anything	everything	something	nothing	either	neither	each	much

Also check pronouns for ambiguity. The following sentence is grammatically incorrect:

> Successful athletes pay attention to their coaches because they know the value of experience.

Who does "they" refer to, the coaches or the athletes? If you can't tell, then the pronoun is ambiguous.

QUICK QUIZ #1

1. If it is not raining <u>on Sunday</u>, Sheila and <u>them</u>
                                 A   B

   <u>are going</u> on <u>a picnic</u> in Hyde Park. <u>No error</u>
      C   D   E

2. Many photographers are coming to believe

   <u>that</u> color prints are <u>as artistic</u> as black
   A   B

   and white ones because <u>they</u> reveal new
                             C

   definitions <u>of art</u>. <u>No error</u>
             D   E

3. Computers may or <u>may not be</u> <u>superior to</u>
                       A   B

   typewriters; after all, <u>they</u> have a steady
                              C

   power source <u>and</u> extreme flexibility.
                 D

   <u>No error</u>
     E

4. While many cooking experts hold that the only

   <u>proper</u> way to bake a potato is in a conventional
   A

   oven, others contend that <u>cooking</u> <u>them</u> in a
                            B   C

   microwave is a <u>perfectly</u> acceptable alternative.
                   D

   <u>No error</u>
     E

Answers and Explanations: Quick Quiz #1

1. **B** The issue here is pronoun case. Always check underlined pronouns for ambiguity, agreement, and case errors. "Sheila and them" are the subject of the sentence, which means that you need the subject pronoun "they" instead of "them." A good way to see this error is to remove the other subject noun, "Sheila," and read the sentence again.

2. **C** This is a pronoun ambiguity question because "they" could refer to photographers, color prints, or black and white prints.

3. **C** Ambiguity again. "They" could refer to computers or typewriters. The sentence is additionally confusing because one could argue that both machines have a "steady power source and extreme flexibility."

4. **C** The pronoun "them" (plural) refers to the noun "potato" (singular). Remember to check pronouns for agreement with the nouns they replace.

VERB ERRORS

When you see a verb underlined, check to make sure it agrees with its subject. Also, make sure all the verbs in the sentence are in the proper tense.

QUICK QUIZ #2

1. Last year, <u>as</u> in years past, the majority of
            A

   candidates <u>are dropping</u> out of the race
               B

   before the actual election because they no

   longer <u>had</u> the funds or the will <u>to campaign</u>.
         C   D

   <u>No error</u>
      E

2. Restrictions on one of the committees that

   <u>monitors</u> corporate waste disposal
     A

   <u>were revoked</u>, <u>allowing</u> the committee
       B   C

   <u>to levy</u> fines on violators of the disposal laws.
      D

   <u>No error</u>
      E

3. The Lipizanner <u>stallion, a breed of horses that nearly went extinct at the end of World War II, are featured</u> in performances at the Hofburg Palace in Vienna.

   (A) stallion, a breed of horses that nearly went extinct at the end of World War II, are featured
   (B) stallion, a breed of horses which came very close to going extinct at the end of World War II, is featured
   (C) stallion, nearly going extinct at the end of World War II the breed of horses was, are featured
   (D) stallions, a breed of horses which nearly went extinct at the end of World War II, is featured
   (E) stallions, a breed of horses that nearly went extinct at the end of World War II, are featured

ANSWERS AND EXPLANATIONS: QUICK QUIZ #2

1. **B** The sentence is in the past tense, as indicated by "last year." "Are dropping" is wrong because it's in the present tense.

2. **A** The verb "monitors" is singular, while "committees," the subject of the verb, is plural.

3. **E** The subject in the original is "stallion," which takes a singular verb, but here it is paired up with "are." Eliminate choices A and C due to this error. Choice D changes "stallion" to "stallions," while changing the verb to "is," so you still end up with an agreement error. Choice B uses "which" in a restrictive, essential phrase, which requires using "that."

OTHER MINOR ERROR TYPES

ETS may also test your knowledge of a few other minor grammar problems. If you don't spot a pronoun or verb error, check for the following:

- **Idioms** are combinations of words that must be used in conjunction. For example, the phrase "responsible for" is an idiom; you wouldn't say "responsible of." If you see a preposition underlined, check to see if it's used idiomatically.

- **Diction** errors are errors in word choice. These are hard to spot, but fortunately don't show up too often. Look for these only after you've determined that there are no grammatical errors.

COMMON IMPROVING-SENTENCES ERRORS

Many of the errors found in the error identification questions will also show up in the improving sentences questions. However, there are a few error types that are more common to the improving sentences question type.

DANGLING MODIFIERS

A dangling modifier has no specific word that it modifies. Take a look at the following sentence:

1. Running down the street, a brick fell on my head.

In this sentence, the modifier is "running down the street," but the noun directly after it is "a brick." It appears that the brick is running down the street, not the person. Make sure your modifiers refer to the correct noun.

This sentence should be rewritten as something like this:

1. As I was running down the street, a brick fell on my head.

PARALLEL CONSTRUCTION

When making a list of items, make sure all parts of the list are in the same form. The following sentence is incorrect:

1. Ricky wanted to finish his homework, take a walk, and to be in bed by ten o'clock.

The correct form would be the following:

1. Ricky wanted to finish his homework, take a walk, and be in bed by ten o'clock.

If you are making a comparison, make sure the two things being compared are similar.

1. John's drumming style is more explosive than Keith.

This sentence is incorrect because it compares John's *drumming style* to *Keith.* You should compare John's *drumming style* to Keith's *drumming style.*

QUICK QUIZ #3

1. Highly sociable animals living in pods that are fairly fluid, <u>dolphin interactions with other dolphins from other pods is fairly common</u>.

   (A) dolphin interactions with other dolphins from other pods is fairly common
   (B) dolphins commonly interact with other dolphins from other pods
   (C) dolphins interact commonly with other dolphins from other pods
   (D) dolphin interactions with other dolphins from other pods are a common phenomenon
   (E) dolphins can be found commonly interacting with other dolphins from other pods

2. In the 1970s, American youngsters primarily listened to rock music, while in the current decade, <u>anything goes</u>.

   (A) anything goes
   (B) the kids like anything
   (C) they listen to a diverse blend of styles
   (D) many styles appeal to youngsters
   (E) they like almost anything

Answers and Explanations: Quick Quiz #3

1. **B** The original sentence contains a misplaced modifier; dolphin interactions are not highly sociable animals, and "interactions" is plural, so the verb "are" (not "is") should be used. Choice D repeats the misplaced modifier error, so eliminate it. In choice C, "interact commonly" describes the way they interact, which is not the intended meaning. In choice E, "commonly interacting" describes the way they interact—not the intended meaning, which is that they interact often.

2. **C** If a sentence compares two things, verify that it compares apples to apples in a parallel way. This sentence is comparing *what youngsters listened to in the 1970s to what youngsters listen to in the current decade.* Choice C correctly completes the comparison by identifying what "they listen" to in the current decade. In choices B and E, what they *listened to* is compared to what they *like.* Choices A and D are bad comparisons because the subject has become the musical styles, whereas the original subject was the listeners.

How to Eliminate Answers on Improving Sentences

When in doubt, use the following guidelines to help you eliminate answers. These guidelines should be applied only after you're stuck or are down to two or three choices.

Avoid answer choices that

1. contain the word "being" or other "-ing" verbs

2. are wordy or redundant

3. contain unnecessary or ambiguous pronouns

4. change the meaning of the sentence

IMPROVING PARAGRAPHS QUESTIONS

For these questions, you will work with a rough draft of an essay. You will be asked not only to fix grammatical errors of the type we've already looked at, but also to revise sentences, add transitions, and add or delete sentences. Just as with critical reading, go right to the questions. You don't get any points for reading the essay. On the test, six questions from 30–35 will follow a passage like the one you see below.

Here's an example.

(1) Clothing can be made from many different types of substances. (2) There are two main groups of fibers: natural and man-made. (3) Some natural fibers are cotton, wool, and linen and some man-made fibers are polyester, rayon, and nylon, and the difference depends on look and feel.

(4) Many people prefer to wear natural fibers because they feel more natural against the skin. (5) You sweat and perspire less because the cloth is organic and breathes. (6) However, it feels good on the body, but cotton and linen can wrinkle more easily.

(7) Artificial fibers tend to make a person sweat more because they are composed of having a plastic base. (8) Plastic does not breathe very much like a plastic rain poncho. (9) But because plastic is man-made, it is easier than natural cloth to get it to do what one wants. (10) Because we don't like wrinkly clothes, we make artificial fabrics that stay and remain wrinkle-free.

(11) So if one wants to look ironed and crisp all day, wear man-made clothes. (12) But if one prefers the comfort and feel of aeration and a perspiration-free feeling, choose natural fibers. (13) Determining whether you're a style or a texture person determines which fabrics you'll prefer. (14) If you cannot decide, try a blend!

1. Which of the following is the best revision of sentence 5 (reproduced below)?

   You sweat and perspire less because the cloth is organic and breathes.

   (A) The wearer perspires less because the organic cloth breathes.
   (B) The cloth ends sweating and perspiring because it is organic and breathes.
   (C) Organic, breathing cloth prevents sweating and perspiring.
   (D) One never sweats while wearing cloth that is organic and breathes.
   (E) Cotton and polyester prevent perspiration.

2. In context, which of the following sentences placed before sentence 7 best connects the second paragraph to the third?

(A) Unlike natural fabrics, man-made fabrics wrinkle less, but they do not feel as pleasant on the body.

(B) Cotton and linen are not man-made fibers and, consequently, behave differently.

(C) Nevertheless, all fibers have their advantages, especially man-made fibers.

(D) Some fibers encourage perspiration, a healthy, cleansing process of the skin.

(E) However, appearance is more important than feel, so man-made clothes are preferable.

3. In context, where would sentence 13 (reproduced below) be better placed within the essay?

Determining whether you're a style or a texture person determines which fabrics you'll prefer.

(A) Before sentence 12
(B) Before sentence 11
(C) Before sentence 2
(D) After sentence 14
(E) Before sentence 6

REVISION QUESTIONS

When revising sentences, first make sure that there are no grammatical errors. Then pick the answer that is concise and does not change the meaning of the sentence. You should also use the Process of Elimination guidelines for improving sentences to aid you.

Let's return to question 1 from the previous page.

1. Which of the following is the best revision of sentence 5 (reproduced below)?

You sweat and perspire less because the cloth is organic and breathes.

(A) The wearer perspires less because the organic cloth breathes.

(B) The cloth ends sweating and perspiring because it is organic and breathes.

(C) Organic, breathing cloth prevents sweating and perspiring.

(D) One never sweats while wearing cloth that is organic and breathes.

(E) Cotton and polyester prevent perspiration

Eliminate choices C, D, and E because they change the meaning of the sentence. Choice B has an ambiguous pronoun. Take it out. You're left with answer choice A, the best answer.

TRANSITION QUESTIONS

For transition questions, go back to the passage and read the sentences before and after the one you're going to work with. Determine what direction the sentences are going in—do they maintain the same flow of ideas or do they change the topic? When adding a transition sentence, do not go off the topic or add any new information.

2. In context, which of the following sentences placed before sentence 7 best connects the second paragraph to the third?

   (A) Unlike natural fabrics, man-made fabrics wrinkle less, but they do not feel as pleasant on the body.
   (B) Cotton and linen are not man-made fibers and, consequently, behave differently.
   (C) Nevertheless, all fibers have their advantages, especially man-made fibers.
   (D) Some fibers encourage perspiration, a healthy, cleansing process of the skin.
   (E) However, appearance is more important than feel, so man-made clothes are preferable.

Read sentences 6 and 7. Sentence 6 is about man-made fabrics while sentence seven is about artificial ones. So, we've introduced a new idea. Look for the choice that best expresses this change in topic. Choice A looks like the winner.

CONTENT QUESTIONS

Some questions require you to work more with the content of the essay. You may need to rearrange sentences or provide a title for the essay. Read only as much as you need to answer these questions.

3. In context, where would sentence 13 (reproduced below) be better placed within the essay?

   Determining whether you're a style or a texture person determines which fabrics you'll prefer.

   (A) Before sentence 12
   (B) Before sentence 11
   (C) Before sentence 2
   (D) After sentence 14
   (E) Before sentence 6

Take a look at sentence 13. What is it about? Now, read the sentences in the answer choices and use the Process of Elimination to get rid of answers that aren't similar in topic. Putting sentence 13 before 12 makes little sense; it separates the two examples. It certainly shouldn't be placed near sentences 2 or 6, either. How about before sentence 12? That works. Sentence 13 discusses two considerations: style and texture. Sentences 11 and 12 then give example of these two considerations; thus, choice B is best.

GRAMMAR: PROBLEM SET 1

Directions: The following sentences test your knowledge of grammar, usage, word choice, and idiom.

Some sentences are correct.

No sentence contains more than one error.

You will find that the error, if there is one, is underlined and lettered. Elements of the sentence that are not underlined will not be changed. In choosing answers, follow the requirements of standard written English.

If there is an error, select the <u>one underlined part</u> that must be changed to make the sentence correct and fill in the corresponding oval on your answer sheet.

If there is no error, fill in oval Ⓔ .

EXAMPLE:

<u>The other</u> delegates and <u>him</u> <u>immediately</u>
   A   B   C

accepted the resolution <u>drafted by</u> the
                      D

neutral states. <u>No error</u>
             E

1. The teacher <u>noted</u> that the inspired writing
         A
Joe displayed on his <u>homework</u> was
               B
<u>incompatible to</u> the prosaic prose <u>he produced</u>
    C   D
in class. <u>No error</u>
        E

2. The well-manicured lawns, the marble columns,

and the <u>fountains that were impressive</u>
           A
<u>indicated</u> this <u>was no</u> ordinary <u>summer cottage</u>.
 B   C   D
<u>No error</u>
 E

3. Considering the blinding snowstorm <u>and</u>
                        A
ice-covered roads, you and <u>her</u> <u>were</u> lucky
                B   C
<u>to arrive</u> here safely. <u>No error</u>
 D   E

4. Although <u>its</u> flavor is <u>derided</u> <u>by connoisseurs</u>,
       A   B   C
the popularity of milk chocolate is <u>far greater</u>
                          D
than that of dark chocolate. <u>No error</u>
                 E

5. Eager to reach the widest audience <u>possible</u>,
                        A
the popular group ABBA recorded songs not

only in <u>their</u> native Swedish <u>but also</u> in a
     B   C
<u>number of</u> other languages. <u>No error</u>
 D   E

6. To celebrate the 1976 <u>bicentennial, classes</u>
                    A
from each local school <u>attended</u> a grand
               B
fireworks display and, <u>having</u> never seen such
               C
a sight, <u>was amazed</u> by the beauty. <u>No error</u>
      D   E

Answers and Explanations: Problem set 1

1. **C**   Always check prepositions for idioms. The correct idiom is "incompatible with."

2. **A**   This sentence contains a parallelism error. Remember to check that any items in a list are the same part of speech—and if the list contains verbs, then check that those verbs are in the same tense. Because the sentence lists "well-manicured lawns" (an adjective and noun) and "marble columns" (an adjective and noun), the phrase "fountains that were impressive" (noun, verb, and adjective) is not parallel. The phrase correctly written would be "...and the impressive fountains..."

3. **B**   This sentence contains a pronoun case error. The use of the pronoun "her" is incorrect because it is the subject of the sentence and "her" is an object pronoun. A good way to see this error is to remove the other subject noun, "you," and read the sentence again. The correct word is the subject pronoun, "she."

4. **A**   This is a pronoun ambiguity question because "its" could refer to popularity, milk chocolate, or dark chocolate. Because you don't know which is correct, the pronoun is ambiguous.

5. **B**   The pronoun "their" (plural) refers to the collective noun ABBA (singular). Remember to check pronouns for agreement with the noun they replace and, yes, collective nouns are singular.

6. **D**   The verb "was amazed" is singular, but the subject is "classes," which is plural. Ignore the extra information in the middle of the sentence when checking for subject-verb agreement.

GRAMMAR: PROBLEM SET 2

Directions: The following sentences test your knowledge of grammar, usage, word choice, and idiom.

Some sentences are correct.

No sentence contains more than one error.

You will find that the error, if there is one, is underlined and lettered. Elements of the sentence that are not underlined will not be changed. In choosing answers, follow the requirements of standard written English.

If there is an error, select the one underlined part that must be changed to make the sentence correct and fill in the corresponding oval on your answer sheet.

If there is no error, fill in oval Ⓔ.

EXAMPLE:

The other delegates and him immediately
   A   B   C

accepted the resolution drafted by the
                             D

neutral states. No error
             E

SAMPLE ANSWER

1. Visitors to the zoo have often looked into
                        A

   exhibits designed for lions and saw ducks or
                          B

   crows eating treats or enjoying water intended
      C   D

   for the large cats. No error
               E

2. Before the sun rose yesterday, Rebecca
            A

   has already awoken and begun her morning
   B   C

   regimen of activities. No error
   D   E

3. Jill knows that she performs worse on multiple-
                      A

   choice tests than on short answer tests, where
         B   C

   she is required to show her understanding
                  D

   in writing. No error
          E

4. Each member of the audience told the director
                     A

   that the thriller was the scariest movie that
                B

   they had ever seen. No error
  C   D   E

Directions: The following sentences test correctness and effectiveness of expression. In choosing answers, follow the requirements of standard written English; that is, pay attention to grammar, choice of words, sentence construction, and punctuation.

In each of the following sentences, part of the sentence or the entire sentence is underlined. Beneath each sentence you will find five ways of phrasing the underlined part. Choice A repeats the original; the other four are different.

Choose the answer that best expresses the meaning of the original sentence. If you think the original is better than any of the alternatives, choose it; otherwise choose one of the others. Your choice should produce the most effective sentence—clear and precise, without awkwardness or ambiguity.

EXAMPLE: SAMPLE ANSWER

Laura Ingalls Wilder published her first book
<u>and she was sixty-five years old then</u>.

(A) and she was sixty-five years old then
(B) when she was sixty-five
(C) at age sixty-five years old
(D) upon the reaching of sixty-five years
(E) at the time when she was sixty-five

---

5. In the summer, the Ruddy Duck <u>male, who lives in marshes, have</u> chestnut colored plumage and its bill is blue, but in the winter, the male is brown with a creamy colored face.

   (A) male, who lives in marshes, have
   (B) male was living in marshes and has
   (C) male that lives in marshes, it has
   (D) male lives in marshes with its
   (E) male, which lives in marshes, has

6. To be a good psychologist, one must <u>be trustworthy, kind, and a patient listener,</u> or else one's clients will not feel comfortable.

   (A) be trustworthy, kind, and a patient listener,
   (B) be trusted, kind, and be patiently listening,
   (C) be trustworthy, kind, and patient as a listener,
   (D) be trusted, have kindness, and also be a patient listener,
   (E) have trust, kindness, and be a patient listener,

ANSWERS AND EXPLANATIONS: PROBLEM SET 2

1. **B** "Have…looked" is correct, but "have…saw" is not. Rather, the correct verb tense is "seen."

2. **B** The verb "has already awoken" is in the present perfect tense, but the sentence is referring to something that happened in the past, before yesterday's sunrise. The past perfect tense, "had already awoken," is required.

3. **C** Use the word "where" only to refer to places; in this sentence it incorrectly refers to "short answer tests."

4. **C** The pronoun "they" (plural) incorrectly refers to the noun "member" (singular).

5. **E** Choice A incorrectly uses "who" to refer to an animal and contains a subject-verb error; choice B incorrectly introduces the past tense into the sentence; choice C changes the meaning of the sentence by suggesting that the description applies only to Ruddy Duck males that live in the marshes; choice D makes it sound as if the duck lives with its plumage.

6. **C** In a list of three or more things, always check for parallelism. Choice C is the most consistent and concise, providing a list of three adjectives. Choices A and E have a list that mixes verbs with nouns. Choice B is not consistent because it uses "be" on only the first and third items in the list. Choice D is consistent, but longer and more awkward than is choice C.

GRAMMAR: PROBLEM SET 3

Directions: The following sentences test your knowledge of grammar, usage, word choice, and idiom.

Some sentences are correct.
No sentence contains more than one error.

You will find that the error, if there is one, is underlined and lettered. Elements of the sentence that are not underlined will not be changed. In choosing answers, follow the requirements of standard written English.

If there is an error, select the <u>one underlined part</u> that must be changed to make the sentence correct and fill in the corresponding oval on your answer sheet.

If there is no error, fill in oval Ⓔ.

EXAMPLE:

<u>The other</u> delegates and <u>him</u> <u>immediately</u>
  A   B   C

accepted the resolution <u>drafted by</u> the
                         D

neutral states. <u>No error</u>
              E

<u>SAMPLE ANSWER</u>

Ⓐ ● Ⓒ Ⓓ Ⓔ

---

1. <u>Accept</u> for chocolate <u>desserts</u> in restaurants,
  A   B

   I generally avoid eating <u>sugar, cake, and candy</u>
                            C

   in order to stay <u>healthy</u>. <u>No error</u>
               D   E

2. <u>Although</u> pennies seem to be cheap and
  A

   inconsequential donations, charities <u>agree</u>
                          B

   that <u>it</u> adds <u>up to</u> a significant sum. <u>No error</u>
     C   D   E

3. Against the advice of <u>their</u> coach, <u>who</u> <u>has led</u>
                    A   B   C

   many teams to victory, this year's baseball

   team attended more parties than practices and

   <u>had</u> an especially disappointing season.
  D

   <u>No error</u>
  E

4. Neither the ongoing costs associated with

   <u>feeding</u> so many tigers nor the difficulties
  A

   caused by meddling neighbors

   <u>has been considered</u> prior <u>to purchasing</u> the
         B   C

   the land and <u>building</u> the sanctuary.
            D

   <u>No error</u>
  E

Directions: The following sentences test correctness and effectiveness of expression. In choosing answers, follow the requirements of standard written English; that is, pay attention to grammar, choice of words, sentence construction, and punctuation.

In each of the following sentences, part of the sentence or the entire sentence is underlined. Beneath each sentence you will find five ways of phrasing the underlined part. Choice A repeats the original; the other four are different.

Choose the answer that best expresses the meaning of the original sentence. If you think the original is better than any of the alternatives, choose it; otherwise choose one of the others. Your choice should produce the most effective sentence—clear and precise, without awkwardness or ambiguity.

EXAMPLE:

Laura Ingalls Wilder published her first book and she was sixty-five years old then.

(A) and she was sixty-five years old then
(B) when she was sixty-five
(C) at age sixty-five years old
(D) upon the reaching of sixty-five years
(E) at the time when she was sixty-five

SAMPLE ANSWER

5. Impractical for cold climates, Ashley decided against packing her flip-flops for her vacation in Alaska.

(A) Impractical for cold climates,
(B) Because she was impractical for cold climates,
(C) They are impractical, since the climate is cold, so
(D) Because they are impractical for cold climates,
(E) Since the cold climate is impractical for them,

6. Nick's friends enjoyed spending time talking to his mother, unlike spending time with Manny's.

(A) spending time with Manny's
(B) spending time talking to Manny's mother
(C) spending time with Manny's mother
(D) talking to Manny
(E) talking to Manny's household

Answers and Explanations: Problem Set 3

1. **A**   Here, the author uses incorrect diction. The word "accept" means "to receive" something offered. The author should have chosen "except," which means "to the exclusion of." If you missed this one, don't sweat it. Diction errors are rare.

2. **C**   This pronoun agreement question has the singular word "it" referring to the plural words "pennies" and "donations."

3. **A**   Here is another collective noun. The pronoun "their" (plural) incorrectly refers to the collective noun "team" (singular).

4. **B**   The verb "has been considered" is singular, but it should agree with "difficulties." When you use "neither...nor" or "either...or," the verb must agree with the noun following "nor" or "or."

5. **D**   The sentence intends to say that flip-flops are impractical for cold climates, so Ashley didn't pack hers. Choice D uses the plural pronoun "they," which correctly refers to "flip-flops." Choice A has an introductory phrase with no subject, so it makes "Ashley" the thing that is impractical for cold climates. Choice B also makes Ashley the impractical element. Choice C is awkwardly arranged. Choice E changes the intended meaning of the original sentence.

6. **B**   Choice B is correct because the comparison is between talking to either Nick's mother or Manny's. Choices A and D are incorrect because they compare talking to Nick's mother to Manny himself. Although Choice C might be considered correct in that it compares Nick's mother to Manny's mother, it should be eliminated because it changes the meaning. Choice E is eliminated because it compares one person to a group of people.

GRAMMAR: PROBLEM SET 4

Directions: The following sentences test your knowledge of grammar, usage, word choice, and idiom.

Some sentences are correct.
No sentence contains more than one error.

You will find that the error, if there is one, is underlined and lettered. Elements of the sentence that are not underlined will not be changed. In choosing answers, follow the requirements of standard written English.

If there is an error, select the <u>one underlined part</u> that must be changed to make the sentence correct and fill in the corresponding oval on your answer sheet.

If there is no error, fill in oval Ⓔ.

EXAMPLE:

<u>The other</u> delegates and <u>him</u> <u>immediately</u>
   A   B   C

accepted the resolution <u>drafted by</u> the
                          D

neutral states. <u>No error</u>
              E

SAMPLE ANSWER

Ⓐ ● Ⓒ Ⓓ Ⓔ

1. Either the United States <u>or</u> the Philippines <u>is</u>
                       A   B

the top <u>choice of</u> the State Department
           C

<u>to receive</u> the mining contract. <u>No error</u>
   D   E

2. Anyone <u>seeking to</u> get in shape, <u>regardless of</u> a
            A   B

ge or ability, can benefit from <u>having</u> a
                         C

personal trainer show <u>them</u> the best approach.
                   D

<u>No error</u>
  E

3. <u>Though</u> popular mainly as a device that
   A

played music, Edison's phonograph <u>is</u>
                                B

originally created <u>as</u> an educational tool
                C

to teach spelling and <u>allow</u> deaf people to
                      D

to hear recordings of books. <u>No error</u>
                          E

Directions: The following sentences test correctness and effectiveness of expression. In choosing answers, follow the requirements of standard written English; that is, pay attention to grammar, choice of words, sentence construction, and punctuation.

In each of the following sentences, part of the sentence or the entire sentence is underlined. Beneath each sentence you will find five ways of phrasing the underlined part. Choice A repeats the original; the other four are different.

Choose the answer that best expresses the meaning of the original sentence. If you think the original is better than any of the alternatives, choose it; otherwise choose one of the others. Your choice should produce the most effective sentence—clear and precise, without awkwardness or ambiguity.

EXAMPLE:

Laura Ingalls Wilder published her first book and she was sixty-five years old then.

(A) and she was sixty-five years old then
(B) when she was sixty-five
(C) at age sixty-five years old
(D) upon the reaching of sixty-five years
(E) at the time when she was sixty-five

SAMPLE ANSWER

4. Notwithstanding having spent several hours in meetings with each other and with an arbitrator, the parties were unable to reach an agreement.

(A) Notwithstanding having spent several hours
(B) Notwithstanding several hours to be spent
(C) Although the parties spend several hours
(D) Notwithstanding to have spent several hours
(E) Although the spending of several hours

5. Once considered revolutionary and controversial, the movements of impressionism and abstract expressionism have steadily gained popularity; its images can now be found on drugstore postcards.

(A) have steadily gained popularity; its images can now be found on drugstore postcards
(B) have steadily gained popularity; impressionist images can now be found on drugstore postcards
(C) has steadily gained popularity; and so images can now be found on drugstore postcards
(D) has steadily gained popularity, and its images can now be found on drugstore postcards
(E) have steadily gained popularity; their images are now founded on drugstore postcards

6. Alien species piggybacking on human travelers to new countries are wreaking havoc on planet Earth, though they live for only a short time.

(A) wreak havoc on planet Earth, though they live for only a short time
(B) are wreaking havoc on planet Earth, though they are living for only a short time
(C) are wreaking havoc on planet Earth, though the alien species live for only a short time
(D) are wreaking havoc on planet Earth and live for only a short time
(E) are wreaking havoc on planet Earth and though the species live for only a short time

ANSWERS AND EXPLANATIONS: PROBLEM SET 4

1. **E** The subject is "either" and takes the singular verb "is." Countries are collective nouns and thus take a singular verb.

2. **D** The pronoun "them" (plural) does not agree with the pronoun "anyone" (singular). Remember to check pronouns for agreement with the nouns they replace.

3. **B** The error in this sentence occurs at choice B, which is an inappropriate verb form. To match the past tense established and used elsewhere in the sentence ("played," "created"), the past tense "was" is needed.

4. **A** Although "notwithstanding" sounds clumsy, there is no error in the sentence as written. Try not to pick choices just because they sound bad. Look for identifiable errors. Choices B, C, and D are in the wrong tense. Choice E turns "spending" into a noun, so the first phrase lacks a verb and makes no sense.

5. **B** The sentence is ambiguous; "it" could refer to abstract expressionism or impressionism. Choice B clarifies the ambiguity. Choices C and D incorrectly use a singular verb (the subject is "movements"). Choice E is incorrect: one can find the images on postcards, but the images are not founded on (i.e., based on) the postcards.

6. **C** The original sentence contains an ambiguous pronoun; it is unclear who "they" is referring to. Choice B repeats this error; eliminate it. Choice D changes the meaning of the sentence: It no longer contrasts the fact that they wreak havoc with the fact that they live for only a short time. Choice E clears up the ambiguity but in doing so creates a sentence fragment.

GRAMMAR: PROBLEM SET 5

Directions: The following passage is an early draft of an essay. Some parts of the passage need to be rewritten.

Read the passage and answer the questions that follow. Some questions are about particular sentences or parts of the essay or the entire essay and ask you to consider organization and development. In making your decisions, follow the conventions of standard written English. After you have chosen your answer, fill in the corresponding oval on your answer sheet.

Questions 1-6 are based on the following student essay.

(1) In these days of pollution, you must clean one's car with something other than rain. (2) There are many car washing techniques available and they have their pluses and minuses.

(3) First, one type of car wash is the touch-free car wash that a lot of people like because it doesn't scratch the paint on one's car. (4) Basically it's a stream of water at a really high force like a fire hose's pressure. (5) But not everybody likes touch-free because it might not get off really tough dirt and stains. (6) Scrubbing is necessary.

(7) The traditional car wash with the waving strips of cloth touches one's car, it might scratch it, especially if the cloth strips still have attached bits of dirt or gravel from the last car. (8) But the strips can rub the stains out more successfully with friction and water and soap instead of just water and soap.

(9) The best type of car wash is to wash by hand if you have the time. (10) Although this takes up a lot of time, you can get out all the dirt without scratching your car if one is careful and thorough. (11) Car washing by hand is a better idea in the summer or one will freeze.

1. Which of the following is the best version of sentence 3 (reproduced below)?

   First, one type of car wash is the touch-free car wash that a lot of people like because it doesn't scratch the paint on your car.

   (A) The touch-free car wash is a favorite type of car wash among people who do not like their cars' paint scratched.
   (B) Many people prefer the touch-free car wash because it does not scratch car paint.
   (C) Although the touch-free car wash scratches car paint, many prefer it.
   (D) People who do not like scratched car paint will like the touch-free car wash because it does not scratch car paint.
   (E) Many people like the touch-free car wash that is preferred because it does not scratch the paint on cars.

2. In context, which of the following sentences placed before sentence 7 best connects the second paragraph to the third?

   (A) For a scrubbing function, do not use a touch-free car wash.
   (B) Nevertheless, a touch-free car wash has other advantages.
   (C) Therefore, scrub a car to avoid scratching.
   (D) Because a stream of water is never enough to cut through dirt, one should avoid a touch-free car wash.
   (E) For tougher dirt, one should use a car wash that physically scrubs the car.

3. The writer's main rhetorical purpose of the essay is to

(A) explore the advantages and disadvantages of different car washing methods
(B) explain how pollution causes dirty cars and thus must be controlled
(C) establish that touch-free is the best type of car wash because it does not scratch a car's paint
(D) show how to wash a car quickly and well by hand
(E) illustrate that hand washing is the superior form of car washing during the winter

4. Which of the following is the best revision of the underlined portion of sentence 8 (reproduced below)?

But the strips can rub the stains out more successfully <u>with friction and water and soap instead of just water and soap</u>.

(A) with friction, water, and soap instead of just water and soap
(B) with friction and soap instead of just water
(C) with soap added to friction instead of just water
(D) with friction added to the standard soap and water mixture
(E) with soap and water instead of just friction

5. In context, which revision would most improve sentence 10 (reproduced below)?

Although this takes up a lot of time, you can get out all the dirt without scratching your car if one is careful and thorough.

(A) Change "Although" to "Because."
(B) Delete "up a lot of."
(C) Change "get out" to "remove."
(D) Change "one is" to "you are."
(E) Add "in one's work" after "thorough."

6. If the essay were to continue after sentence 11, which of the following would be the best content for sentence 12?

(A) However, there are many advantages to each method of car washing.
(B) Depending on the newness of a car, one can determine which car washing method is most effective.
(C) Essentially, car owners have many types of car washing methods to choose from, and their preferences will determine the truly best car wash.
(D) In conclusion, one should choose a sunny, warm day for the cleaning endeavor so that the car being washed will not develop water spots.
(E) Only if a car owner has time is hand washing the best method for cleaning a car.

Answers and Explanations: Problem Set 5

1. **B** Choices A and D perpetuate the original sentence's problem with repetition. Choice C changes the meaning of the original sentence. Choice E is wordy. Choice B is the best choice because it retains the full meaning of the sentence while conveying the thought concisely.

2. **E** Choice C changes the meaning of the paragraphs. Choices A, B, and D focus too much on the touch-free car wash. A sentence added to the beginning of the third paragraph should lead into the topic of that paragraph: the traditional car wash. Because choice E focuses more on the traditional car wash, it is the best choice.

3. **A** Choice B is mentioned but is not the main purpose. Choice C states that the author prefers touch-free car washing; however, the essay refutes this declaration. Choice D is incorrect because the author explains that one cannot hand wash a car well without time. Choice E is disproved by the last sentence. Choice A is the best choice because it encompasses the whole essay.

4. **D** Choices B, C, and E alter the meaning of the original sentence. Choice A looks appealing, but it still has a lot of repetition. Choice D is the best option because it is the most concise without the redundancy problem.

5. **D** This change needs to be made to fix an incorrect switch from the second person pronoun "you" to the third person pronoun "one." Choice A indicates that this sentence would support the prior sentence, but it is intended to be a contrast. Choices B and C make acceptable changes, but the original versions are also acceptable so it isn't much of an improvement. Choice E makes the sentence longer than it needs to be, since the original version is acceptably clear.

6. **C** The last sentence of any essay should draw together all the thoughts presented as a conclusion. Choice A mentions only the positives, not the negatives. Choice B introduces a new idea, the newness of a car, instead of summarizing the essay. Choice D sums up only the last paragraph and brings in the new concept of water spots. Choice E repeats only sentences 9 and 10.

GRAMMAR: PROBLEM SET 6

Directions: The following passage is an early draft of an essay. Some parts of the passage need to be rewritten.

Read the passage and answer the questions that follow. Some questions are about particular sentences or parts of the essay or the entire essay and ask you to consider organization and development. In making your decisions, follow the conventions of standard written English. After you have chosen your answer, fill in the corresponding oval on your answer sheet.

Questions 1-6 are based on the following passage.

(1) I don't think that people living near an active volcano should be forced to move to a safer home. (2) Let me explain why they should be permitted to keep their homes.

(3) First of all, many people think a volcano is a dangerous place to live but there are plenty of active volcanoes in the world with whole cities around them and plenty that haven't exploded in centuries. (4) Sometimes an active volcano just drizzles out lava. (5) Other places have their own potential problems like living on the coast is dangerous for hurricanes, living in the Midwest is dangerous for tornadoes, and living in lower elevated areas is dangerous for flash flooding. (6) People should learn to face their fears because they can never move to a truly safe place.

(7) Secondly, people should be allowed to live where they choose. (8) If someone wants to live on a volcano, maybe they have a good view or a fertile garden. (9) Maybe they live near their families and friends. (10) Maybe they have a house that has been in their family for generations. (11) The government should not force them to move because of the possibility of disaster. (12) They have something precious that is worth sustaining all these scary possibilities for: a home.

1. Which of the following is the best revision of the underlined portion of sentence 3 (reproduced below)?

   First of all, many people think a volcano is a dangerous place <u>to live but there are plenty of active volcanoes in the world with whole cities around them and plenty that haven't exploded</u> in centuries.

   (A) (as it is now)
   (B) to live; accordingly, there are many active volcanoes surrounded by cities that have not exploded in centuries
   (C) to live, although many active volcanoes have remained quiet for centuries in order to encourage cities to grow
   (D) to live, including the quiet, citified ones
   (E) to live. However, many of the world's active volcanoes are surrounded with cities and have remained quiet for centuries

2. In context, which of the following words should be placed at the beginning of sentence 5 (reproduced below)?

   Other places have their own potential problems like living on the coast is dangerous for hurricanes, living in the Midwest is dangerous for tornadoes, and living in lower elevated areas is dangerous for flash flooding.

   (A) Furthermore
   (B) Consequently
   (C) Although
   (D) Subsequently
   (E) However

3. Which of the following words best replaces the underlined word in sentence 6 (reproduced below)?

   People should learn to <u>face</u> their fears because they can never move to a truly safe place.

   (A) View
   (B) Acknowledge
   (C) State
   (D) Address
   (E) Represent

4. The writer's main rhetorical purpose of the essay is to

   (A) advocate for the rights of those who chose to live on volcanoes
   (B) urge the government to instate stricter housing regulations on and around volcanoes
   (C) support the idea that home is a state of mind rather than a geographic location
   (D) offer that daredevils substitute dangerous places to live
   (E) demonstrate how the general populace is composed of cowards

5. In context, which words should be placed at the beginning of sentence 11 (reproduced below)?

   The government should not force them to move because of the possibility of disaster.

   (A) Despite these realities
   (B) For all these reasons
   (C) Misunderstanding their excuses
   (D) Against these justifications
   (E) Escalating these tenets

6. In context, which would be the best place to insert the following sentence?

   Slow, predictable lava flow is not much of a hazard.

   (A) After sentence 2
   (B) After sentence 4
   (C) After sentence 6
   (D) After sentence 7
   (E) After sentence 10

Answers and Explanations: Problem Set 6

1. **E** Choice A is very wordy. Choices B and D say that the second half of the sentence is a continuation of the first half. However, in the original sentence, the second half opposes the first. Choice C may seem appealing, but it personifies the volcano, giving it the ability to choose to let cities grow by not exploding.

2. **A** Choices C and E mean the opposite of "also," the word you need for this transition. Choices B and D mean that this sentence follows the previous one in sequence. However, this sentence does not directly follow the idea of drizzling lava. Instead, it adds another point to the whole argument. Therefore, choice A is the best choice.

3. **D** Choices A, C, and E have different meanings from "face." Choice B seems attractive, but the sentence is looking for people to do more than acknowledge their fears. Therefore, choice D is the best answer.

4. **A** Choices B and C oppose the main point of the essay. Choices D and E make assumptions not stated in the essay. Choice A best summarizes the gist of the essay.

5. **B** Choices A, C, and D incorrectly state that this sentence will be different, rather than include, the previous sentences. Choice E may seem like a good option, but there are no "tenets" mentioned in this paragraph. Therefore, choice B is best.

6. **B** Sentence 4 describes how some active volcanoes merely drizzle out lava, implying that they are therefore not very dangerous. This new sentence would explicitly make that point. Choice A would start the author's rationale too early, since sentence 3 begins *first of all*. Choice C follows a sentence about facing fears, whereas the new sentence is suggesting there is little to fear. Choices D and E relate to why people want to live near a volcano. This new sentence relates to why people do not need to fear living near a volcano, which was discussed in the second paragraph.

On the following pages, you will find a practice Grammar section, similar to what you will find on the SAT. Give yourself exactly 25 minutes to complete this test section. Good luck!

NO MATERIAL ON THIS PAGE.

SECTION 6
Time — 25 minutes
35 Questions

Turn to Section 6 of your answer sheet to answer the questions in this section.

Directions: For each question in this section, select the best answer from among the choices given and fill in the corresponding circle on the answer sheet.

The following sentences test correctness and effectiveness of expression. Part of each sentence or the entire sentence is underlined; beneath each sentence are five ways of phrasing the underlined material. Choice A repeats the original phrasing; the other four choices are different. If you think the original phrasing produces a better sentence than any of the alternatives, select choice A; if not, select one of the other choices.

In making your selection, follow the requirements of standard written English; that is, pay attention to grammar, choice of words, sentence construction, and punctuation. Your selection should result in the most effective sentence—clear and precise, without awkwardness or ambiguity.

Example:

Laura Ingalls Wilder published her first book <u>and she was sixty-five years old then</u>.
(A) and she was sixty-five years old then
(B) when she was sixty-five
(C) at age sixty-five years old
(D) upon the reaching of sixty-five years
(E) at the time when she was sixty-five

Ⓐ Ⓑ Ⓒ Ⓓ ●

1. Americans vote for an electoral college, not a president, <u>since such is the case, a candidate can win the popular vote but still lose the election</u>.

   (A) since such is the case, a candidate can win the popular vote but still lose the election
   (B) and a candidate can win the popular vote but still lose the election because of that
   (C) a candidate can win the popular vote but still lose the election as a result
   (D) a candidate can win the popular vote but still lose the election for this reason
   (E) so a candidate can win the popular vote but still lose the election

2. Gabriel García Márquez's novel *One Hundred Years of Solitude* had the same influence <u>as James Joyce's *Ulysses* also did</u>: Both books changed the way we approach literature.

   (A) as James Joyce's *Ulysses* also did
   (B) as that which James Joyce's *Ulysses* also did
   (C) as James Joyce's *Ulysses* did
   (D) like that which James Joyce's *Ulysses* did
   (E) like that of James Joyce's *Ulysses* did

3. <u>The requirements for becoming an astronaut is</u> knowledge of physics and physical fitness rather than simple bravery and a sense of adventure.

   (A) The requirements for becoming an astronaut is
   (B) An astronaut, it requires
   (C) The job of an astronaut requires
   (D) In becoming an astronaut is required
   (E) As for becoming an astronaut

4. The survivor of poverty and child abuse, <u>her show deals with Oprah's recovery as well as the spiritual growth of her viewers</u>.

   (A) her show deals with Oprah's recovery as well as the spiritual growth of her viewers
   (B) Oprah's recovery and the spiritual growth of her viewers is the subject of her show
   (C) the subject of her show is Oprah's recovery as well as the spiritual growth of her viewers
   (D) Oprah deals with her recovery as well as the spiritual growth of her viewers on her show
   (E) Oprah, whose show deals with her recovery as well as the spiritual growth of her viewers, discusses this on her show

GO ON TO THE NEXT PAGE

5. <u>Winning medal after medal at the Olympic Games in 1984, Mary Lou Retton's gymnastic abilities delighted her coaches.</u>

(A) Winning medal after medal at the Olympic Games in 1984, Mary Lou Retton's gymnastic abilities delighted her coaches.

(B) Winning medal after medal at the Olympic Games in 1984, Mary Lou Retton delighted her coaches with her gymnastic abilities.

(C) With winning medal after medal at the Olympic Games in 1984, Mary Lou Retton's gymnastic abilities delighted her coaches.

(D) Mary Lou Retton, winning medal after medal at the Olympic Games in 1984, her coaches were delighted with her gymnastic abilities.

(E) The winning of medal after medal at the Olympic Games in 1984 delighting Mary Lou Retton's coaches, thanks to her gymnastic abilities.

6. <u>Wild bears, when surprised in their natural habitats, can be violent,</u> the best course of action is to avoid bears altogether.

(A) Wild bears, when surprised in their natural habitats, can be violent,

(B) Wild bears, surprising in their natural habitats, can be violent, therefore

(C) Wild bears, when surprised in their natural habitats, can be violent, however

(D) Because wild bears, when surprised in their natural habitats, can be violent,

(E) When wild bears, surprised in their natural habitats, can be violent,

7. <u>Los Angeles's freeways, usually busier and more crowded than those of other cities,</u> are clogged almost twenty-four hours a day, contributing to the city's pollution problem.

(A) Los Angeles's freeways, usually busier and more crowded than those of other cities,

(B) The freeways of Los Angeles, which are usually busier and more crowded with cars than other cities,

(C) The freeways of Los Angeles, usually busier and more crowded than other cities,

(D) The freeways of Los Angeles, usually busier and crowding with cars than other cities,

(E) Usually busier and more crowded than other cities, the freeways of Los Angeles

8. <u>Because the pioneers had to travel across hostile lands, encountering weather, illness, and injury is the reason why</u> many were reluctant to make the journey.

(A) Because the pioneers had to travel across hostile lands, encountering weather, illness, and injury is the reason why

(B) Because the pioneers had to travel across hostile lands, encountering weather, illness, and injury,

(C) Pioneers had to travel across hostile lands, encountering weather, illness, and injury and is the reason why

(D) As a result of having to travel across hostile lands, encountering weather, illness, and injury

(E) The fact that the pioneers had to travel across hostile lands, encountering weather, illness, and injury is why

9. Set in the sixteenth <u>century, modern audiences enjoyed the contemporary opera *Galileo, Galilei* written by Philip Glass.</u>

(A) century, modern audiences enjoyed the contemporary opera *Galileo, Galilei* written by Philip Glass

(B) century and written by Philip Glass, modern audiences enjoyed the contemporary opera *Galileo, Galilei*

(C) century, the contemporary opera *Galileo, Galilei* was written by Philip Glass and enjoyed by modern audiences

(D) century, Philip Glass's contemporary opera *Galileo, Galilei* has enjoyed great success with modern audiences

(E) century, Philip Glass wrote the contemporary opera *Galileo, Galilei* which enjoyed great success with modern audiences

GO ON TO THE NEXT PAGE ⟩

10. Eating cholesterol-rich foods is one of the lead-ing causes of high <u>cholesterol; another</u> equally damaging is a lack of exercise.

   (A) cholesterol; another
   (B) cholesterol, another one that is
   (C) cholesterol, the other that is
   (D) cholesterol; another one which is being
   (E) cholesterol, another cause that is

11. <u>Whenever television is denounced by viewers for its violence, they call</u> on the department of Standards and Practices to take action.

   (A) Whenever television is denounced by viewers for its violence, they call
   (B) Whenever television is denounced by viewers calling on its violence,
   (C) Whenever television is denounced for its violence, viewers call
   (D) Whenever viewers denounce television for its violence, they call
   (E) Whenever a denunciation of television is voiced, they call

GO ON TO THE NEXT PAGE

The following sentences test your ability to recognize grammar and usage errors. Each sentence contains either a single error or no error at all. No sentence contains more than one error. The error, if there is one, is underlined and lettered. If the sentence contains an error, select the one underlined part that must be changed to make the sentence correct. If the sentence is correct, select choice E. In choosing answers, follow the requirements of standard written English.

Example:

The other delegates and him immediately
    A   B   C

accepted the resolution drafted by the
                             D

neutral states. No error
            E

Ⓐ ● Ⓒ Ⓓ Ⓔ

12. The vegetarian movement in this country, which

has shown increasing growth over the last thirty
               A   B

years, was begun at a farm in Wheaton, Vermont,
        C

in the late 1800's. No error
D   E

13. Although they have radically different career
    A   **B**

plans, Luna and Gabriel both hope to be
                         C

a Michigan State graduate one day. No error
          D   E

14. Ever since his promotion to manager last year,
              A

John is the hardest-working employee of this
      B   C

small and highly industrious company. No error
          D   E

15. Even though a promotion might be a
    A

somewhat easy method for a store to boost sales,
    B   C

they may lead some people to shop irresponsi-
D

bly. No error
   E

16. To create a pasta with a richer egg flavor, Martha
    A

urged her audience to separate the egg whites
      B

with the egg yolks. No error
C   D   E

17. Like many other forms of social organization,
          A

a commune functions smooth only as long as
       B   C

everyone works together. No error
      D   E

18. Before Homecoming Weekend, Lucia and Kiki

took time to study for the upcoming finals, but
A

as a result of the game and many parties, she
  B   C

needed to study again. No error
D   E

19. Only infrequently did James laugh at the jokes
  A

that the comedian has been telling; James simply
          B

did not find the comedian's punch lines, none

of which seemed original, to be funny. No error
  C   D   E

20. One of the most imminent dangers to the
           A

Kemp's ridley turtle, the smallest of all sea turtles,
                      B

is that the female nests only on a small stretch
                    C

of beach in Mexico that is now the target of
D

developers. No error
  E

21. Widespread wildfires followed by heavy rains can
  A

result in mudslides, which have harmful affects
  B   C

on the environment. No error
D   E

GO ON TO THE NEXT PAGE →

22. It is difficult for my friends <u>and I</u>
                                    A
<u>even to contemplate</u> <u>playing</u> chess against some-
        B   C
one accused <u>of cheating</u>. <u>No error</u>
              D   E

23. The existence of consistent rules <u>are</u> important <u>if</u>
                                       A   B
a teacher wants <u>to run</u> a classroom <u>efficiently</u>.
                  C   D
<u>No error</u>
    E

24. Students in the literature course will explore

ways <u>in which</u> Medieval authors <u>represented</u>
      A   B
themes of their time, and <u>will have read</u> Augus-
                            C
tine's *Confessions*, Boccaccio's *Decameron*, and

<u>Heloise and Abelard's</u> *Letters*. <u>No error</u>
          D   E

25. When <u>one is</u> sitting in a crowded theater,
          A
surrounded by an audience that <u>has</u> paid
                                 B
good money to see a play of such historical

significance, the least you can do <u>is</u> <u>refrain from</u>
                                     C   D
unnecessary conversation. <u>No error</u>
                             E

26. No matter how many times a person <u>has driven</u>
                                        A
in inclement weather, <u>they should</u> be <u>especially</u>
                        B   C
careful when driving down a road <u>that</u> is cov-
                                    D
ered with wet snow. <u>No error</u>
                       E

27. <u>By the time</u> the composer was <u>considered successful</u>,
    A   B
he <u>had already</u> published numerous <u>symphonies</u>.
      C   D
<u>No error</u>
    E

28. <u>When</u> Dr. Jantos speaks, <u>she</u> does not attempt
    A   B
<u>to impress</u> her <u>listeners with her speaking</u>.
    C   D
<u>No error</u>
    E

29. After <u>engaging</u> in a spirited debate, everyone
            A
except <u>Andrea and I</u> <u>decided</u> to watch the latest
        B   C
action film, even though the rest of the group had

<u>already seen</u> it. <u>No error</u>
    D   E

GO ON TO THE NEXT PAGE ⟹

Directions: The following passage is an early draft of an essay. Some parts of the passage need to be rewritten.

Read the passage and select the best answers for the questions that follow. Some questions are about particular sentences or parts of sentences and ask you to improve sentence structure or word choice. Other questions ask you to consider organization and development. In choosing answers, follow the requirements of standard written English.

Questions 30-35 are based on the following passage.

(1) After eating gelato in Italy in Florence, I was amazed that it was not sold in America. (2) Gelato is Italian ice cream, but its smoother and fluffier than ours. (3) Some American cities do have gelato shops also called gelaterias and some ice cream manufacturers produce processed gelato. (4) Neither tastes like Italian gelato. (5) I decided to try to figure out why the flavors and textures differ. (6) I decided to make my own gelato.

(7) I discovered that gelato is very, very hard to make well. (8) First, it needs to have some air by churning it in to make it fluffy, but not too much air because too much air would make it too fluffy. (9) Stores and manufacturers add things like emulsifiers to keep things fluffy long term. (10) Gelato in Italy is made and eaten on the same day so the texture does not need artificial and chemical preservatives.

(11) Flavors of American versions of gelato were bland in comparison in order to mass-produce ice cream of any sort American producers find it easier to use frozen canned or otherwise preserved fruits. (12) By highly processing fruits and other ingredients, they lose a lot of flavor. (13) Italian producers purchase just enough fresh fruit to make the day's batch of gelato.

(14) In conclusion, gelato does not work in America because it's nature prevents it from mass production. (15) Good gelato must be created correctly, in the Italian way, in small batches and using the freshest ingredients.

30. In context, which is the best word to insert before the underlined portion of sentence 4 (reproduced below) to connect this sentence to the rest of the first paragraph effectively?

    Neither tastes like Italian gelato.

    (A) However
    (B) Consequently
    (C) Additionally
    (D) Subsequently
    (E) And

31. In context, which of the following is the best version of sentences 5 and 6 (reproduced below) ?

    I decided to try to figure out why the flavors and textures differ. I decided to make my own gelato.

    (A) In order to make my own gelato, I decided to discern why the flavors and textures differ.
    (B) The flavors and textures differ, so I attempted to create my own gelato.
    (C) In order to determine why the flavors and textures differ, I decided to make my own gelato.
    (D) Since the flavors and textures differ, I decided to find out why.
    (E) My gelato illustrated why the flavors and textures differ.

32. The writer's main rhetorical purpose in the essay is to

    (A) advertise for Florentine ice cream
    (B) describe the process of creating gelato
    (C) explain the narrator's obsession with gelato production
    (D) illustrate why Italians eat gelato on the day of its creation
    (E) show why Italian gelato is superior to American gelato

GO ON TO THE NEXT PAGE

33. In context, which of the following is the best revision of sentence 8 (reproduced below) ?

    First, it needs to have some air by churning it in to make it fluffy, but not too much air because too much air would make it too fluffy.

    (A) First, one fluffs gelato by churning it carefully to ensure the perfect quantity of air is added.
    (B) To make gelato fluffy, one must churn in air and watch the texture so that too much air is not churned in.
    (C) By expanding gelato's fluffiness, one is careful to avoid air.
    (D) Too much air transforms gelato into ice cream; one can avoid this by churning.
    (E) One can churn air into gelato for fluffiness; beware excess air which makes the gelato overly fluffy and incorrect.

34. In sentence 9, "things" is best replaced by

    (A) stuff
    (B) ingredients
    (C) processes
    (D) objects
    (E) manufacturers

35. In context, which of the following is the best revision of sentence 14 (reproduced below) ?

    In conclusion, gelato does not work in America because it's nature prevents it from mass production.

    (A) (As it is now)
    (B) Since gelato does not work in America because its nature prevents it from mass production.
    (C) However, gelato is not possible in America because its nature makes it difficult to mass-produce.
    (D) In conclusion, American manufacturers cannot make authentic-tasting gelato because by nature it's difficult to mass-produce.
    (E) Being that American manufacturers cannot make authentic-tasting gelato because by nature its difficult to mass-produce.

STOP
**If you finish before time is called, you may check your work on this section only.
Do not turn to any other section in the test.**

NO TEST MATERIAL ON THIS PAGE.

GO ON TO THE NEXT PAGE

PRACTICE SECTION:
ANSWERS AND EXPLANATIONS

1. **E** Choice A, Choice B, and Choice D all have awkward constructions. Choice C is a run-on sentence.

2. **C** Choice A uses the word *also*, which is redundant after *as*. Choice B adds the unnecessary words *that which*, as well as the redundant *also*. Choice D and Choice E use the wrong comparison word *like*.

3. **C** The subject in Choice A, *the requirements*, needs a plural verb. Choice B and Choice D are awkward. Choice E lacks a subject, making it a sentence fragment.

4. **D** Choice A, Choice B, and Choice C do not put the subject of the modifier, *The survivor of poverty and child abuse*, right after the comma where it belongs. Choice E is awkward.

5. **B** Choice A and Choice C say that Retton's abilities were winning the events, not Mary Lou Retton herself. Choice D and Choice E are sentence fragments.

6. **D** Choice D correctly makes the beginning into a clause, so the sentence is no longer a run-on. Choice A, Choice B, and Choice C are run-on sentences. Choice E changes the meaning of the sentence.

7. **A** Choice B, Choice C, and Choice E have a parallelism problem. The freeways of Los Angeles should be compared with the freeways of other cities, not the cities themselves. Choice D incorrectly uses the phrase *crowding with cars*.

8. **B** Choice A, Choice C, and Choice E make the error of using a singular verb *is* to refer to *lands, weather, illness*, and *injury*. Choice D never identifies the subject of the sentence, *pioneers*, and *because* is better construction than *as a result of having to*.

9. **D** Choice A and Choice B are constructed so that the audiences, rather than the opera, are set in the sixteenth century. Choice C employs the passive voice, which is not as strong as the active voice of Choice D. Choice E sets Philip Glass in the sixteenth century.

10. **A** Choice B, Choice C, and Choice E are run-on sentences. Choice D corrects the run-on problem but is awkwardly wordy and uses the *-ing* form of *is*.

11. **D** Choice A, Choice B, Choice C, and Choice E are in the passive voice. Choice D is the only choice that is not passive.

12. **C** If you remove the clause between the commas (*which...years*) you are left with *The vegetarian movement in this country was begun at a farm....* The verb *was begun* is passive and awkward. The movement began once and the action is completed so we should use the simple past tense "began."

13. **D** The subject *Luna and Gabriel* is plural. *A Michigan State* graduate needs to agree with this subject in number but is singular as written. It should be *Michigan State graduates.*

14. **B** Always check that verbs are in the correct tense. The verb *is* is in the simple present tense, yet the context tells us that John was promoted last year and has been a hard worker ever since. To indicate that an action began in the past and continues to the present, use the present perfect tense, "has been."

15. **D** Remember to check that pronouns agree in number with the noun they replace. The pronoun *they* is plural. It replaces the noun *promotion*, which is singular. Therefore, the use of *they* is incorrect.

16. **C** In the correct idiom, the word *separate* should be followed with the preposition *from*. Although *separate* is not right next to its preposition, the rule still applies.

17. **C** *Smooth* is in adjectival form here, but it is modifying the verb *functions*, so it should be an adverb, "smoothly."

18. **C** The sentence includes two singular females (*Lucia and Kiki*). Therefore, the pronoun *she* is ambiguous.

19. **B** The verb *has been telling* (present perfect tense) needs to be the same tense as the verb *did* (past tense). It is therefore incorrect (and should be replaced with "told").

20. **E** There are no errors in the sentence as it is written.

21. **C** *Affects* is usually a verb meaning "to have an influence on," while a noun is needed in the sentence. Therefore, "effects" should be used here to mean "something brought about by a cause or agent; a result."

22. **A** Remember to check that the pronouns are in the correct case. Should the pronoun be *I* or *me*? To see this clearly, remove the other part of the phrase, *my friends and*. Is the correct sentence "It is difficult for I" or "It is difficult for me"? "Me" is correct.

23. **A** Make sure verbs agree with their subjects. The verb is *are*, which is plural. The subject is *existence*. Notice you can take the phrase *of consistent rules* out of the sentence and the sentence still makes sense. This means that *rules* cannot be the subject. Because *existence* is singular and *are* is plural, Choice A is wrong.

24. **C** The verb *will explore* is in the future tense. *Will have read* describes an action that takes place before another action. Because there is no other action that follows, it should be changed to the future tense "will read."

25. **A** The pronoun in the first part of the sentence (*one*) has to be the same as the pronoun in the second part (*you*). Because *you* isn't underlined (and thus can't be changed), our only option is to replace *one is* with "you are."

26. **B** The plural pronoun *they* refers to the singular noun *person* and is therefore incorrect. It should be replaced with "he or she."

27. **E** There are no errors in the sentence as it is written.

28. **D** The sentence is wordy and redundant. Choice D should simply say "listeners."

29. **B** Prepositions like *except* should be followed by the object case; thus, "except Andrea and me" is the correct phrasing.

30. **A** Choice B, Choice C, Choice D, and Choice E suggest that sentence 4 stems from the prior sentences as a natural conclusion. However, sentence 4 opposes the previous sentences, so Choice A, *however*, is the best option. Understanding this sentence requires understanding these transition words.

31. **C** Choice A is awkward and questionable in meaning. Choice B is close, but leaves out the causal relationship between the sentences, the "why." Choice D, although concise, leaves out the second sentence. Choice E implies the gelato-making experiment was successful, but this is not supported by the text.

32. **E** Choice A may have happened inadvertently, but it is not the writer's *main rhetorical purpose*. Choice B is not supported by the text. Choice C is incorrect because *obsession* is extreme and unjustified. Choice D is in the text, but it is not the main purpose of the essay.

33. **A** Choice B is still awkward and wordy; it also ends in a preposition. Choice C is incorrect because one is aiming to add air, not avoid it. Choice D is wrong because ice cream is not mentioned. In Choice E, the person speaking changes halfway through the sentence; the first clause is in the third person and the second clause is in the second person command form. Choice E also has unnecessary repetition at the end.

34. **B** Choice A is too informal; Choice B is a better choice. Choice C, Choice D, and Choice E aren't things that could be added to the gelato.

35. **D** The original sentence is awkward in two places (*gelato does not work in America* and *prevents it from mass production*) and contains a diction error (*it's*, which means "it is"). Choice B becomes a sentence fragment when *Since*, a word that introduces a dependent clause, replaces *In conclusion*. Also, Choice B corrects only the diction error and does not fix the awkward phrases in the original. The first awkward phrase is replaced by an equally awkward one in Choice C, and the word *However* incorrectly indicates a change of direction in the sentence or a contrast to the previous idea. Both Choice D and Choice E replace both awkward phrases with clearer ones: *gelato does not work in America* becomes *American manufacturers cannot make authentic-tasting gelato*, and *by nature prevents it from mass production* becomes *by nature it's difficult to mass produce*. However, Choice E introduces the sentence with *Being that*, which makes the sentence a fragment, and incorrectly uses *its* to mean "it is." Only Choice D corrects all the errors without adding others.

6

The Essay

THE ESSAY

The first section of the SAT will give you 25 minutes to write an essay. ETS will provide you with a brief excerpt, usually no more than about 80 words, often, but not always, from a literary work. This prompt will touch on some issue or perspective, and you will be asked to present your views on the subject.

Your essay will be graded by two readers and will receive a raw score between 2 and 12. This score counts for about 30 percent of your final Writing section score. But don't worry. Writing an essay for a standardized test is a piece of cake, provided you know what qualities are being looked for by ETS.

WRITING THE ETS WAY

Guess how much time is spent reading each essay before assigning a grade. Ten minutes? Nope. Five minutes? Not quite. One to two minutes. And each reader is allowed to read your essay only once. In that amount of time, there's no way the reader can absorb every little detail of your essay. Instead, the reader judges your essay holistically, looking to see if your essay does the following:

1. **Does your essay answer the question?** You have to write your essay on the prompt provided, no matter how dull or uninteresting that topic may be. Make sure you stick to the topic throughout your paper.

2. **Is your essay well-organized?** Make sure your essay contains an introduction paragraph, body paragraphs, and a conclusion. Use nice, clear transitions between topics.

3. **Does your essay make use of specific examples?** Use specific examples to back up your thesis.

4. **Is your essay free of grammatical mistakes?** You don't have to be a top writer to get a great score on the essay. Keep things simple, and avoid the kind of errors found in the grammar section.

PARTS OF THE ESSAY

THE PROMPT

Here is an example of a typical essay prompt:

Directions: Consider carefully the following excerpt and the assignment below it. Then plan and write an essay that explains your ideas as persuasively as possible. Keep in mind that the support you provide—both reasons and examples—will help make your view convincing to the reader.

> The one constant in human history is change. Whether the change is something as fundamental as the shift from a hunting-and-gathering society to an agricultural society or one as seemingly trivial as the changes in fashion, there is no escaping the mutability of human existence. Clearly, because change is such an inescapable feature of civilization, it must be a good and necessary thing.
>
> **Assignment**: Do you believe that change is a "good and necessary" thing? In an essay, support your position by discussing an example (or examples) from literature, the arts, science and technology, history, current events, or your own experience or observation.

The essay prompt is designed to be fairly open-ended; you should be able to address the topic in a variety of ways. Most likely, you will

1. agree with the prompt

2. agree, but with certain exceptions

3. disagree with the prompt

4. disagree, but with certain exceptions

Of course, it doesn't matter what angle you take on the prompt—there is no right or wrong answer.

THE INTRODUCTION

Your goal in the introduction paragraph is to let the reader know what the topic is and then to tell the reader what you will say in your essay about the topic.

If you use the above prompt, your introductory paragraph could look something like this:

> Change is inevitable fact of life. But is change always for the best? When one considers the potentially dangerous impact of changes such as industrialization and the advent of nuclear technology, it is clear that change, while inescapable, is not always for the best.

That's it. Restate the prompt and then state your thesis.

BODY PARAGRAPHS

Each body paragraph should discuss only one example. Your essay will become muddled if you try to do too much in a paragraph. Use a clear transition to begin the body paragraph. Here are some good ones to try.

However	Even though
While	Moreover
Although	Another example
Furthermore	Secondly
In addition	Despite
Therefore	

Your body paragraph should look something like this:

Although many people might consider industrialization a change for best, think of all the damage to our culture and environment that industrialization has caused. The proliferation of factories has created serious problems with air and water pollution. Additionally, there has been a human cost. The need for workers has led companies to exploit people and use them as cheap labor. While industrialization does provide us with modern conveniences, it is clear that on the whole this change is not entirely for the best.

Notice how the paragraph stays on topic. The examples support the idea that change is not necessarily good. The sentences are clear and direct.

Try to have two or three body paragraphs. Although it is sad to say, the length of your essay is an important factor. Fill up as many of the available lines as you can.

THE CONCLUSION

Your essay must have a conclusion. All you need to do in the conclusion is restate your thesis, like so:

> In light of the above examples, it is clear that change is not always for the best. The examples of industrialization and nuclear technology demonstrate that change, while in some ways beneficial, brings about a number of negative consequences.

PACING ON THE ESSAY

You have 25 minutes for the essay. Spend the first five minutes reading the prompt and brainstorming examples. Try to come up with at least three examples. You may even want to think of general examples before the test. Historical facts, current events, and literature are all good sources of examples for your essay.

Use the next 15 minutes to write your essay. Aim for a five-paragraph essay, with an introduction, three body paragraphs, and a conclusion. Stay focused on the topic, and keep things simple.

Take the last five minutes to proofread your essay. Watch out for grammar mistakes—one or two may be okay, but too many of them will hurt your score. If you're unsure how to spell a word, choose a different one.

The visual appearance of your essay is important, as well. While you should avoid double-spacing or otherwise puffing up your essay, it helps to indent your paragraphs, neatly erase any mistakes, and write as legibly as you can manage. If you make the reader's job easier, you're more likely to get a better score.

ESSAY CHECKLIST

When you are finished with the essay prompts below, check each essay using these criteria. If you want a second opinion, ask a friend, parent, or teacher to grade your essay, as well.

Check your essay for

1. An introduction paragraph. Does your introduction paragraph contain a strong topic sentence, one that lets the reader know what the paper will discuss? Does your introduction paragraph mention what examples your paper will include? Does your introduction paragraph end with a clear thesis statement?

2. Body paragraphs. You should have two to three of these. Does each body paragraph contain a nice clear transition sentence? Does each body paragraph develop one and only one example? Does your example clearly support your thesis statement?

3. A conclusion. Your essay has a conclusion, right? Did you restate your thesis? Did you summarize how your examples support your thesis?

4. Grammar and style. Does your essay contain a minimal amount of grammatical mistakes? Look especially for the types of errors that appear on the error ID and improving sentences questions. Try to avoid

- subject-verb agreement errors. Remember that words like "everyone," "anyone," and "everybody" are singular.

- ambiguous pronouns. Your writing will be much clearer if you keep pronouns to a minimum.

- verb tense errors. Keep all your verbs in the same tense.

5. Now look for stylistic issues. Does your essay contain frequent misspellings? Did you vary the length of your sentences? Are your paragraphs indented? Remember: Neatness counts (somewhat), so strive to write as clearly as possible.

SAMPLE ESSAY PROMPTS

Use the following essay prompts to practice writing under pressure. Give yourself 25 minutes for each prompt.

PROMPT #1

Directions: Consider carefully the following excerpt and the assignment below it. Then plan and write an essay that explains your ideas as persuasively as possible. Keep in mind that the support you provide—both reasons and examples—will help make your view convincing to the reader.

> We have strived at every turn to progress, to always push forward. Regression will not be tolerated, nor will stagnation—perseverance our only guiding principle. We will not be satisfied with anything less than progress, for progress is always positive.
>
> **Assignment**: Do you agree that progress is always positive? In an essay, support your position by discussing an example (or examples) from literature, the arts, science and technology, history, current events, or your own experience or observation.

_____

_____

_____

_____

_____

_____

_____

_____

_____

_____

_____

_____

_____

_____

_____

_____

_____

_____

_____

_____

_____

_____

_____

PROMPT #2

Directions: Consider carefully the following excerpt and the assignment below it. Then plan and write an essay that explains your ideas as persuasively as possible. Keep in mind that the support you provide—both reasons and examples—will help make your view convincing to the reader.

The times that call for immediate action are few and far between. Most situations that arise allow for a prudent analysis of the possible courses of action as well as their consequences. A leader who decides recklessly or in haste is remiss in his or her duties as a leader. A true leader makes decisions only after careful deliberation and consideration.

Assignment: Do you believe it is accurate to say that a true leader makes decisions only after careful consideration? In an essay, support your position by discussing an example (or examples) from literature, the arts, science and technology, history, current events, or your own experience or observation.

Prompt #3

Directions: Consider carefully the following excerpt and the assignment below it. Then plan and write an essay that explains your ideas as persuasively as possible. Keep in mind that the support you provide—both reasons and examples—will help make your view convincing to the reader.

> Up to this point, I had not experienced a challenge of this magnitude. Never before had I felt so assailed from all fronts. It was a test. My character and my will would for the first time be tempered by hardship. I knew at this moment that the quality that would be most instrumental to my success was my sense of patience. Yes, the patience to endure. In moments of strife, there is no more useful quality than patience.
>
> **Assignment**: Which quality do you believe is the most useful during times of difficulty? In an essay, support your position by discussing an example (or examples) from literature, the arts, science and technology, history, current events, or your own experience or observation.

_____

_____

_____

_____

_____

_____

_____

_____

_____

_____

_____

_____

_____

_____

_____

_____

_____

_____

_____

_____

_____

_____

PROMPT #4

Directions: Consider carefully the following excerpt and the assignment below it. Then plan and write an essay that explains your ideas as persuasively as possible. Keep in mind that the support you provide—both reasons and examples—will help make your view convincing to the reader.

> None of this matters…not the money, the job, the house, the car, nothing. What matters is that tree, that flower, that line of ants. What matters is waking up each morning and watching the sunrise. What matters is sitting outside in the rain. Those little things are the ones that matter.
>
> **Assignment**: Do you agree with the claim that it is the little things in life that matter most? In an essay, support your position by discussing an example (or examples) from literature, the arts, science and technology, history, current events, or your own experience or observation.

Prompt #5

Directions: Consider carefully the following excerpt and the assignment below it. Then plan and write an essay that explains your ideas as persuasively as possible. Keep in mind that the support you provide—both reasons and examples—will help make your view convincing to the reader.

> Philosophers are often concerned with how we know things. One position on knowledge posits that in order to appreciate a concept, we must experience its opposite as well. For example, one cannot know what good is until one has encountered evil.
>
> **Assignment**: Is this a valid viewpoint? Do you agree with the claim that one cannot know a concept without knowing its opposite? In an essay, support your position by discussing an example (or examples) from literature, the arts, science and technology, history, current events, or your own experience or observation.

_____

_____

_____

_____

_____

_____

_____

_____

_____

_____

_____

_____

_____

_____

_____

_____

_____

_____

_____

_____

_____

_____

_____

_____

PROMPT #6

Directions: Consider carefully the following excerpt and the assignment below it. Then plan and write an essay that explains your ideas as persuasively as possible. Keep in mind that the support you provide—both reasons and examples—will help make your view convincing to the reader.

America was founded on a paradox. The founding fathers of this country simultaneously stood for rugged individualism and a government by the people and for the people. This contrast has long made the American spirit, to the extent that there is one, one of the most fascinating to sociologists and political scientists. It seems logical that one cannot stand for both individualism and community.

Assignment: Do you agree with the claim that the needs of the individual and the needs of the community must always be at odds? In an essay, support your position by discussing an example (or examples) from literature, the arts, science and technology, history, current events, or your own experience or observation.

_____
_____
_____
_____
_____
_____
_____
_____
_____
_____
_____
_____
_____
_____
_____
_____
_____
_____
_____
_____
_____
_____

PROMPT #7

Directions: Consider carefully the following excerpt and the assignment below it. Then plan and write an essay that explains your ideas as persuasively as possible. Keep in mind that the support you provide—both reasons and examples—will help make your view convincing to the reader.

> These difficult times require sacrifice. They require us to give of ourselves. Each one of us must ask "What is it that I can give?" We all have something that we can contribute, and contribute we must, because there is no more noble act, or more noble calling, than to sacrifice oneself for the good of all.
>
> **Assignment**: Do you believe that sacrifice is the noblest of acts? In an essay, support your position by discussing an example (or examples) from literature, the arts, science and technology, history, current events, or your own experience or observation.

Prompt #8

Directions: Consider carefully the following excerpt and the assignment below it. Then plan and write an essay that explains your ideas as persuasively as possible. Keep in mind that the support you provide—both reasons and examples—will help make your view convincing to the reader.

1. While secrecy can be destructive, some of it is indispensable in human lives. Some control over secrecy and openness is needed in order to protect identity. Such control may be needed to guard privacy, intimacy, and friendship.

2. Secrecy and a free, democratic government, President Harry Truman once said, don't mix. An open exchange of information is vital to the kind of informed citizenry essential to healthy democracy.

Assignment: Do you agree that people need to keep secrets? In an essay, support your position by discussing an example (or examples) from literature, the arts, science and technology, history, current events, or your own experience or observation.

7
Vocabulary

VOCABULARY

From a long-term perspective, the best way to improve your vocabulary is to read. Some teachers and vocabulary books will tell you to read the classics or scholarly journals, but if you aren't interested in these things, then reading will be painful and unpleasant, and you won't end up doing it.

Instead, think of a subject that totally fascinates you. It could be anything: the history of comic books, detective novels, sports, true romances, or biographies of popular movie stars. Believe it or not, there will be at least one book available in your library or bookstore on any subject you can think of.

Your English teacher may be horrified, but reading anything will get you into the habit of reading, as well as expose you to new words.

Of course, you won't know what those words mean unless you look them up. The test writers at ETS use two dictionaries as they assemble words for the SAT: *The American Heritage Dictionary* and *Webster's New Collegiate Dictionary*. We recommend that you buy one of these; you'll need a good dictionary in college anyway. As you read, get into the habit of looking up words you don't know. It's easy to slide over an unfamiliar word, particularly if you understand the rest of the sentence it's in. However, even if you can figure out the author's meaning, make it a point to look up the word.

Some students like to keep small notebooks and pens next to their dictionaries. Whenever they look up words, they write the words down in the notebooks along with two- or three-word definitions. Later they can quiz themselves on the words.

USING THE WORDS YOU KNOW

Research has shown that the most effective way to memorize anything is to use it in some organic way. For example, if you wanted to memorize a recipe for baked chicken, the most effective way to do it would be to cook the recipe several times. If you wanted to memorize your lines for a school play, the best way to do it would be to say your lines out loud a few times with a friend. Probably the least effective way to memorize anything is to stare at it on the printed page.

The best way to remember words is to use them frequently in conversation. You may feel a little self-conscious the first couple of times you try this, but as you get used to it, you will become more brazen. It's actually pretty easy to find an excuse to use new vocabulary words in almost any situation.

For example, here's a word from the Hit Parade, chosen at random: "erratic" (meaning "unpredictably eccentric") and a situation, also chosen at random: You are trying to explain to a parent why you didn't get a good grade on a history test. Here are three ways to use the word:

"Mom, I'm sorry my performance has been a little erratic lately." (Playing for sympathy, but also designed to impress her with an adult-sounding word.)

"My history teacher is just so erratic that I don't know what to study. Last time he tested only material from the class, but this time he tested stuff out of the textbook that we never even talked about." (Don't blame me; it's all the fault of my psychotic history teacher.)

"Dad, I must say I find your concern to be erratic at best. If you wanted me to study for this test, you shouldn't have let me watch television all weekend. (The best defense is a good offense.)

ABOUT THE HIT PARADE

Whether you have a year or a week to prepare for the verbal part of SAT, the best way to start is to learn the words that are most likely to show up on the test. We've taken around 250 of the most often-used words on the SAT and put them together in this chapter. You may be surprised at how many of these words you already know. The SAT does not test esoteric words such as "esurient." Instead, you will find words that a college freshman is likely to need to know (for example: "esoteric." Have you looked it up yet?).

Bearing in mind that the best way to learn words is to use them in conversation, we have organized the words around common situations in which you might find yourself. If you are going to be eating dinner with your family, read the "At the Dinner Table" section first, and then try out a few words on your unsuspecting family. If you are going to a basketball game after school, read the section "At the Game" and then casually drop a few Hit Parade words into your color commentary.

Even if one of these "common" situations does not seem pertinent to you—"On Trial for Your Life" comes to mind—make it a point to learn the words anyway. Time has shown that ETS uses these words frequently.

If you find you can't work all these words into your conversation, there are two other great ways to memorize words.

Mnemonics

Many students find that they remember words best if they come up with images to help them remember. These images are known as mnemonics. For example, one of the students in our SAT course wanted to remember the meaning of hiatus ("a break or lapse in continuity").

So whenever she sees that word, she pretends she's addressing a friend:

"Hi, (long pause) Atus."

Another student in our SAT course wanted to remember the meaning of the word abridge ("to shorten"). Whenever he sees the word, he thinks:

"A short bridge."

It doesn't matter how silly or bizarre your image is, as long as you won't forget it.

FLASHCARDS

Just as running lines will help you to memorize your part in a production of *Death of a Salesman*, going over the words on the Hit Parade again and again will help you to commit them to memory. A good way to accomplish this is to write down the words you want to remember—in a notebook or, even better, on flashcards. Put the word on one side of the card and the definition on the other. By carrying the flashcards around with you, you can quiz yourself in spare moments—riding home from school or waiting for class to begin.

A FINAL WORD

No matter how much you practice the techniques in the other sections of this book, you will not substantially improve your verbal score without learning additional vocabulary. The Hit Parade that follows is hopefully only the beginning.

Almost nothing else that you can do will change people's perception of you as much as using a more erudite vocabulary. It's more effective than plastic surgery and much less expensive.

THE HIT PARADE

AT THE DINNER TABLE

I **abhor** lima beans; they taste awful to me.

Would it be **presumptuous** of me to ask for seconds?

Your **subtle** use of seasonings was just right.

Hey! Don't **hoard** the mashed potatoes at your end of the table.

I think this rib roast is **tainted**; don't eat it!

abhor	to loathe or detest
hoard	to accumulate or stash away
presumptuous	bold to the point of rudeness
subtle	hardly noticeable
taint	to affect with something harmful; contaminate

ON A DIET

No more for me. I'm being **abstemious**.

I'm totally **satiated**. I couldn't eat another bite.

I'm feeling **replete**. No more mashed potatoes for me.

No thanks, more food would be **superfluous**.

No more brussels sprouts; my plate has reached a **plateau**.

I've already had a **surfeit** of dinner. No more, please.

abstemious	sparing in the use of food or drink
plateau	a condition of neither growth nor decline
replete	gorged with food, sated
satiate	satisfy fully
superfluous	unnecessary
surfeit	excess, overindulgence

"WHAT DO YOU WANT TO DO?"
"I DON'T KNOW, WHAT DO YOU WANT TO DO?"

(With these words, you can take indecision to new heights.)

I'm **vacillating** between going to a movie or going to the mall. What about you?

I'm completely **apathetic**. I'll do whatever you want to do.

Well I'm **indifferent** too. I'll do whatever you want to do.

Maybe because we're feeling so **ambiguous**, we should just hang out here.

No, my mental state is too **precarious** to just stay here.

If you're **skeptical** about your mental health, then maybe we should just skip it.

ambiguous	unclear, having more than one meaning
apathy	lack of interest or caring
indifference	lack of interest, feeling or opinion
precarious	unstable, insecure
skeptical	showing doubt and disbelief
vacillation	wavering, going back and forth

SHOPPING

I have a **penchant** for blue suede shoes; I can't have enough!

I have such a **paucity** of clothes that I barely have anything to wear.

Dad, you are such a **philanthropist** with your donations to my shopping funds.

I know you may believe I'm being **prodigal**, but I really need this mp3 player.

Do you think I would be a **spendthrift** if I bought this $100 shirt?

I think this blouse has a lot of **utility**—it goes with everything I own!

This shirt is very **versatile**—you can wear it inside-out too!

paucity	small amount or number
penchant	a strong taste or liking
philanthropist	someone who gives to worthy causes
prodigal	wasteful
spendthrift	a person who spends money wastefully
utility	usefulness
versatile	capable of doing many things well

STRONG WORDS

Kim was known for her honesty and **integrity** and would never **exploit** someone's weaknesses to her advantage.

John knew how hard it was to be a beginner, so he was always ready to teach a **novice**. For this, his friends **revered** him.

Selena had a **yearning** to write a 1,000-page novel, and nothing less would **satiate** her. Sadly, the school newspaper could only print a few hundred words, so she had to **truncate** her story considerably.

Though he tried to resist, Larry **succumbed** to his desire for a triple-chocolate fudge sundae.

After the politician was accused of **slander**, Alexandra decided to **terminate** her work for his campaign.

Even though some people thought it was a laughing matter, James talked about it with extreme **sobriety**.

exemplary	worthy of imitation
exploit	to take advantage of; to use selfishly for one's own ends
integrity	honesty; moral uprightness
novice	a person who is new at something
revere	to regard with awe
satiate	satisfy fully
slander	untruthful spoken attack on someone's reputation
sobriety	being quiet or serious
succumb	to give way to superior force
terminate	bring to an end
truncate	shorten by cutting off
yearning	deep longing

On Trial for Your Life

Your honor, the **defendant** is obviously lying; his nose is getting longer.

I ask that this man's **testimony** about the accident be stricken from the record because it disagrees with mine.

In **rebuttal** of the prosecution's case against me, I would like to call my mother to the stand.

I would like to **debunk** this young woman's claim that I am her mother; I have never seen her before in my life.

He is a known **truant**; last week, he showed up at school only twice.

The governor is going to **repeal** the death penalty, but he wants to wait until after your execution.

If I have steak for my last meal, would that **preclude** my having lobster as well?

The man **swindled** innocent people by persuading them to buy **tracts** of land that were underwater at high tide.

It is **patently** obvious that I won't get a fair trial in this state.

The **tacit** opinion of this court is that you are a crybaby, but of course we wouldn't say that to your face.

It is my **unbiased** and **objective** opinion that you are not good at anything.

The judge has decided to **void** the lower court's decision to set you free and instead send you to jail for 144 years.

My client is basically **innocuous**. He wouldn't harm a fly—unless the fly really provoked him.

We are asking that she be held without bail because she has been **elusive** in the past.

I don't know why you waste your time arguing with me. My reasoning is always **infallible**.

I find your arguments to be **trite**—almost clichés.

I **infer** from your gagging noises that you don't think much of my conclusion.

May I raise one small **quibble**? Your mother wears army boots.

debunk	to expose the falseness of something or someone
defendant	someone who has been accused of committing a crime
elusive	cleverly avoiding or escaping
infallible	unable to be proven wrong
infer	conclude by reasoning
innocuous	causing or intending little or no harm
objective	not affected by personal feelings
quibble	*v*: to make a minor objection *n*: a small objection
patent	obvious, readily visible
preclude	to make impossible
rebuttal	reply to a criticism or challenge
repeal	to take back a law or other decision

swindle	to cheat out of money or property
tacit	implied, not stated outright
testimony	statement in support of something, often under oath
tract	a piece of land
trite	overused, lacking freshness
truant	someone who cuts school or neglects his or her duties
unbiased	without prejudice
void	to invalidate

The "Artsy" Book Report

The **aesthetic** sensibility demonstrated by the writing took my breath away.

I found the book to be so **stylized** that I couldn't empathize with the characters. The central **paradox** of this book is that any publisher would be foolish to print it in the first place.

The author offers a rich **mosaic** of different immigrants' lives all seamlessly bound together.

The meaning of the passage is almost totally **opaque**—we don't understand the character's motivation, or even what happened to her.

Before I comment on the book's themes, I will begin with a long **synopsis** of the plot.

Each **stanza** of the poem contains three lines, none of which rhyme.

My **thesis** is that the author is in search of his inner child; to prove my point I have written this 900-page manuscript.

At the end of the book, the author returns to the scene that began the book, thus giving a pleasing **symmetry** to the work.

The **phenomena** described in the book are less interesting than the unseen forces that produced them.

While it could be said that *Topics in Linguistic Phonetics* is an **esoteric** book, I for one found it to be a good read.

His art was a **synthesis** of ancient Greek and modern styles.

aesthetic	pertaining to beauty
esoteric	known only by a select few
mosaic	a picture made of small pieces of stone or glass
opaque	not transparent, hard to understand
paradox	something that seems to contradict itself
phenomena	occurrences, facts, or observable circumstances
stanza	section of a poem
stylized	in a particular style, often an unrealistic one
symmetry	balanced proportions
synopsis	plot summary
synthesis	the combining of separate parts to form a whole
thesis	unproven theory; long research paper

AT THE GAME

The spirit of the match was **marred** when the home team refused to shake hands with the visitors.

If we are going to win, we have to **obliterate** its defense.

We must **vanquish** the opposing team in the final quarter.

We're behind by 22 points in the fourth quarter; it's looking **ominous**.

The offsetting penalties **nullified** each other.

The personal foul **negated** the touchdown, and the play had to be done over.

I had a **premonition** about this game so I bet my life savings.

The offense is looking **sluggish**—someone had better wake it up.

You know, the cast on his leg has barely affected his **mobility**.

There is **speculation** that he might be traded to the Bulls.

The **supremacy** of our volleyball team was evident as it handily defeated its opponents.

The cheerleaders **synchronized** their movements so that they finished at precisely the same instant.

Lisa was an **unheralded** volleyball player until she won the big game for us; now, of course, we treat her like a star.

The coach was suspended from the NCAA for **unethical** practices.

Its victory over State University was **unprecedented**; in 30 years of competition, State University has always won.

marred	impaired the perfection of
mobility	ability to move or be moved
negate	to destroy the validity of something
nullify	to make invalid or worthless
obliterate	to wipe out, remove all traces
ominous	signaling something evil is about to happen
premonition	a feeling that something is about to happen
sluggish	lacking energy
speculation	the act of thinking about or pondering something
supremacy	the state of being supreme, or having the most power
synchronize	to cause to occur at the same time
unethical	having bad moral principles
unheralded	unnoticed or unappreciated
unprecedented	without parallel
vanquish	overpower an enemy completely

HOMEWORK EXCUSES (MY CANINE DEVOURED IT)

Do not **condemn** me for not doing my homework, Ms. Cornwell! There are **mitigating** circumstances: I felt it would be **detrimental** to my development if I were to be tied down to the mindless **conformity** of such **conventional** homework.

I also thought that so much typing might **exacerbate** the injury to my wrist.

The book was so **opaque** that I didn't understand a word. Moreover, it was so **soporific** that I couldn't stay awake while reading it.

I know this may sound **implausible**, but as an alternative form of homework I wrote a 50-page paper. I know that it contains a few errors—after all, no one is **infallible**.

Not a single bit of it was **plagiarized**; I wrote it all myself. Although it does contain one paragraph that could be considered a **pastiche**.

condemn	to express strong disapproval of
conformity	the act of becoming similar or identical to
conventional	traditional, mundane
detrimental	causing damage or harm
exacerbate	to make worse
implausible	not possible, not imaginable
infallible	unable to be proven wrong
mitigate	to make less severe
opaque	not transparent, hard to understand
pastiche	piece of music, writing, or art combining several different sources or styles
plagiarist	a person who presents someone else's work as his or her own
soporific	causing sleep

RESPONSES TO PARENTS

But Mom, the music is practically **inaudible** right now.

An 11 o'clock curfew is so **provincial**.

or if you really want to impress them...

This punishment is **tantamount** to **persecution**.

Okay, so I didn't take out the garbage, but don't worry; I'll **rectify** the situation tomorrow.

My room is my **sanctuary**. Please leave.

I'm not active; I'm **slothful**.

Please don't **provoke** me now; I'm feeling very **vulnerable**.

I hereby **renounce** all blood-ties to you.

inaudible	too quiet to be heard
persecution	tormenting a person because of his or her beliefs
provincial	having a narrow scope
provoke	anger, arouse, bring to action
rectify	fix, correct
renounce	to give up or put aside
sanctuary	a safe place or a room for worship
slothful	lazy
tantamount	equivalent in effect or meaning
vulnerable	capable of being hurt

WRITING THE COLLEGE ESSAY

There are many examples that testify to my **indomitable** spirit; for example, when I stubbed my toe before a big test, I went right ahead and took that test, even though I was in tremendous pain. I could have gone to the nurse to get an excuse, but my **innate integrity** would not allow me to take the easy way out.

Although I am only 17 years old, I am considered a **pioneer** in microbiology, having made many important discoveries in the field. Indeed, some colleagues have been tempted to call me **omniscient** because I seem to have an almost encyclopedic grasp of the subject matter. However, my modesty always makes me tell them that they must **temper** their hero-worship. After all, even if my genius makes any modesty **superfluous**, I still **strive** to be a regular guy, who just happens to have the **vitality** of a superhero and the **virtue** of Mother Teresa.

indomitable	unable to be subdued or overcome
innate	existing in a person since birth; part of the character of something
integrity	honesty; moral uprightness
omniscient	having complete knowledge
pioneer	*n.* a leader in a field; *v.* to lead the way in a field
strive	try hard, make a major effort
superfluous	unnecessary
temper	to moderate, to make less extreme
virtue	moral excellence
vitality	energy, liveliness

THE JOB INTERVIEW

My worst attribute? I'm too **meticulous**; no detail is too small for me to keep track of.

My work methods are very **methodical** and **systematic**; I always start with task A and then move to task B.

No task is too **mundane** or **monotonous** for me, and I'll always perform it with a smile.

May I ask how much you paid my **predecessor**?

Give me your biggest problems and I'll solve them. I'm very **resourceful**.

I actually like **subordinate** roles; I don't like responsibility.

I see myself as a **utility** player. I can fit into lots of situations. I'm very **versatile**.

Energy? Are you kidding? I have lots of **vigor**. I'm just full of **zeal**.

So, what's the **prevailing** wage at this Gap outlet?

methodical	orderly; having a set system
meticulous	very careful; attentive to details
mundane	ordinary or commonplace
monotonous	boring; unvarying in tone or content
predecessor	a person who precedes another in an office or a position
prevailing	generally accepted; having superior power
resourceful	able to find solutions
subordinate	placed in a lower order or rank
systematic	regular
utility	usefulness
versatile	capable of doing many things well
vigor	energy, vitality
zeal	enthusiasm and intensity

ALTERNATE WORDS FOR "COOL"

"So what do you think of Lisa?"

"She's totally cool."

"Could you be more specific?"

If you think she's clever, "She's **witty**."

If she's clever in a sophisticated sort of way, "She's **urbane**."

If she's clever in a dry sort of way, "She's **wry**."

If she's really lively, "She's **vivid**."

If she's really important, "She's **vital**."

If she's new and different, "She's **novel**."

If her comments are short and to the point, "She's **succinct**."

If she's never ruffled, "She's **serene**."

If she never gives up, "She's **resolute**."

If she can always get out of gym class, "She's **ingenious**."

If she goes beyond all known limits, "She's **transcendent**."

ingenuity	cleverness; originality
novel	original, new, and different
resolute	strongly determined
serene	calm, peaceful
succinct	brief, concise
transcendent	going beyond known limits
urbane	highly sophisticated
vital	full of energy; necessary for life
vivid	sharp, intense; making an impression on the senses
witty	clever or amusing
wry	dryly humorous

YOU'RE IN LOVE WITH HIM/HER, SO YOU HAVE TO TRY TO EXPLAIN HIM/HER TO YOUR FRIENDS

It's not that he can't talk; he's just **taciturn**.

It's not that he doesn't have an opinion; he's just **reticent**.

She didn't insult you on purpose; it was **unwitting**.

He's not **arrogant**; he's just very confident.

It's not that she hates the entire human race; she's just a little **cynical**.

I'm sure it wasn't **deliberate**. It must have been unintentional.

He's not a **dupe**. He's just very naive.

She's not **gullible**. She's just very innocent.

She's not a **miser**; she's just extremely careful with her money.

She's not **obsessive**. She just happens to like arranging her dolls in exact size order.

He's not a **recluse**. He just enjoys his solitude.

It's not that he isn't passionate. He's **stoic**.

He isn't exactly **strident**; he's just a little grating.

It's not that she's **vengeful**; she just never forgets a slight.

I admit he's a little **vociferous**, but to my knowledge, his **tirades** have never broken anyone's eardrum.

She isn't **verbose**; she just uses a lot of words.

She isn't **sullen**; she's mysterious.

He isn't **torpid** or **slothful**; he's just kind of tranquil.

She isn't a **traitor**; she's just not loyal.

It's not that he's unfaithful. He just likes a lot of **diversity**.

It's not that he's **indecisive**; he just has trouble making up his mind.

She isn't **erratic**; she simply has her own way of doing things.

It's not that she has no personality; she is just **tactful**.

She isn't nosy; she's just very **inquisitive**.

We're a great match; her **tranquility** offsets my nervous personality.

She's not unfocused; she just has **vague** career plans.

arrogance	overconfidence
cynicism	the belief that all human action is motivated by selfishness
deliberate	*adj.* intentional, well thought out; *v.* to consider carefully
diversity	the state of having different elements
dupe	a person easily deceived
erratic	unpredictably eccentric
gullible	easily deceived
indecision	inability to decide
inquisitive	curious
miser	one who saves greedily
obsessive	overly preoccupied
recluse	someone who lives in seclusion
reticent	untalkative, shy, reluctant to speak
slothful	lazy
strident	harsh, grating
stoic	not affected by passion or feeling
sullen	sad, sulky
tactful	saying or doing the proper thing
taciturn	being of few words
tirade	a long, harsh, often abusive speech
torpid	without energy, sluggish
traitor	one who betrays a person, cause, or country
tranquillity	calmness, peacefulness
unwitting	unaware
vague	not precise, unclear
vengeful	wanting or seeking revenge
verbosity	the use of too many words
vociferous	loud

BABY-SITTING

Hello, 911? Is there an **antidote** if someone just drank a whole bottle of Maalox?

Young man, your **impudence** is not respectful to someone who is as old as I am.

Young lady, you are **incorrigible**; they are going to lock you up and throw away the key.

Don't write on the wall, Timmy! That magic marker is **indelible**.

You may be your parents' sole **heir**, but if you don't get down from that refrigerator, you won't live to inherit.

Don't **provoke** me, young man.

If you and your sister want to engage in sibling **rivalry**, it's okay with me so long as there are no scars on your bodies.

Jessica screams all night, so I may need something **soporific** to **subdue** my anxiety and get some sleep. . .something strong enough to **stupefy** me.

Don't try to **undermine** my authority!

You **wily** little brat. I can tell you're still awake.

antidote	remedy for a poison
heir	a person who inherits another's belongings
impudence	bold disrespect or rudeness
incorrigible	not capable of being reformed
indelible	incapable of being erased
provoke	anger, arouse, bring to action
rivalry	an ongoing competition
soporific	causing sleep
stupefy	to make less alert
subdued	quiet, controlled, lacking in intensity
undermine	to injure or destroy underhandedly
wily	artful, cunning, deceitful, sly

ALTERNATE WORDS FOR "BOGUS"

"So what do you think of Dave?"

"He's totally bogus."

"Could you be more specific?"

If he's narrow-minded, he's just very **parochial**.

If he just doesn't matter, he's **irrelevant**.

If he's really ordinary, he's **mediocre** or **mundane**.

If he's got nothing to offer, he's **meager**.

If he's really boring, he's **monotonous**.

If he's gloomy, he's **morose**.

If he's been superseded by someone else, he's **obsolete**.

If he's no longer relevant, he's **extraneous**.

If he has no moral principles, he's **unethical**.

If he makes you nervous, he's **unnerving**.

If he's lacking freshness, he's **trite**.

If he's not in good taste, he's **unseemly**.

If he's not a solid character, he's **unsound**.

If he isn't a serious person, he's **superficial**.

If no one knows who he is, he's **obscure**.

extraneous	not pertinent or relevant
irrelevant	not necessary or important to the matter at hand
meager	lacking in amount or quality; poor
mediocrity	ordinariness; lack of distinction
monotonous	boring; unvarying in tone or content
morose	gloomy; ill-tempered
mundane	ordinary or commonplace
obscure	not known; difficult to understand
obsolete	outdated
parochial	having a narrow scope
superficial	near the surface; slight
trite	overused, lacking freshness
unseemly	unbecoming
unsound	not solid; not well founded; not healthy
unethical	having bad moral principles
unnerving	upsetting; causing nervousness

MEETING ROYALTY

Well, your highness, it's been a **tumultuous** year what with all the scandals.

Are you planning to disinherit any of your **heirs**?

Do you **sanction** your son's behavior?

Have you considered imposing **sanctions** on your son's behavior?

I hear that to be queen of England you have to be willing to wear **ghastly** clothes.

When a **monarch** has relatives like yours, it must be tough to keep your sense of humor.

The constant **lampoons** in the newspapers must be very hard to laugh at when you are their subject.

With the King's death, I imagine there is very little **levity** in the palace right now.

Tell me, your highness, has anyone tried to **usurp** the throne lately?

I've never met such a **lofty magnate** as yourself. Could I have your autograph?

Actually, I'm very **prominent** in Omaha, Nebraska; everybody knows me there.

Long may you **reign**, but could I have that scepter when you kick the bucket?

Are you thinking of **repudiating** your claim to rule America?

Would you take a picture of me posing with this **sentinel**?

These journalists seem to be **ubiquitous**; can't you get rid of them?

ghastly	shockingly frightful
heir	a person who inherits another's belongings
lampoon	sharp satire
levity	lightness; lacking seriousness
lofty	having great height or a stately manner
magnate	a person of great influence in a particular field
monarch	a ruler; a king, queen, or emperor
prominent	standing out, important
reign	*n.* having supreme power; *v.* to rule
repudiate	to cast off or disown; to refuse to acknowledge
sanction	*v.* to give permission; *n.* a coercive measure designed to make a person or persons comply
sentinel	a guard, a watchman
tumultuous	characterized by a noisy uproar
ubiquitous	being everywhere at the same time
usurp	to seize power by force

GETTING RELIGION

The two religious sects have gone in **divergent** directions, but they still meet twice per year in Rome to try to **reconcile** their differences.

The **tenets** of his faith included turning the other cheek.

The **theologian** had been studying religion for more than 20 years.

She was a **pious** person who spent much time in prayer.

The **fundamental** beliefs of the church have not changed in 500 years.

Having been raised in an agnostic household, he was unfamiliar with religious **jargon**.

There was great **lamentation** when the Buddhist priest died.

In a recent **purgation**, one religious **sect** was invited to leave the main body because of doctrinal differences.

Many religions portray hell as a huge **conflagration** that will burn for all eternity.

conflagration	a widespread fire
divergent	moving in different directions from a common point
fundamental	basic, essential
jargon	words used by people in a particular field of work
lamentation	an expression of sorrow or deep regret
pious	having reverence for a god
purgation	the process of getting rid of impurities
reconcile	to settle a problem
sect	a subgroup of a religion; faction
tenet	idea or belief
theologian	one who studies religion

How to Succeed in Business

Your **proposal** for a new headquarters is too expensive.

Our board of directors voted **unanimously** against the proposal.

We were **uniform** in our hatred of your plan.

Our **agenda** now is to find an alternate proposal.

Using both proposals would be **redundant**.

The **blueprint** for our new building calls for 40 stories.

This is a **comprehensive** plan that covers every eventuality.

We do not want the government to **regulate** our industry. We prefer to police ourselves.

We hope that the **stimulus** of a cash infusion will turn our company profitable.

Our results are **verifiable**; an accounting firm has gone over our books and pronounced them accurate.

Our results are not **theoretical**; they are based on hard evidence.

There may be some **residual** ill-feeling from our workers after we cut their salaries by 40 percent.

agenda	a schedule of a meeting
blueprint	a detailed outline or plan for a building
comprehensive	including everything; complete
proposal	an offer or consideration for acceptance
redundant	characterized by unnecessary repetition of words or ideas
regulate	to control or direct by some particular method
residual	describing the part left over
stimulus	something that causes a reaction
theoretical	not proven true, existing only as an idea
unanimity	complete agreement
uniform	alike, identical
verifiable	able to be proven true

THE HIT PARADE (IN ALPHABETICAL ORDER)

abhor	to loathe or detest
abridge	to shorten
abstemious	sparing in the use of food or drink
aesthetic	pertaining to beauty
agenda	a schedule of a meeting
ambiguous	unclear; having more than one meaning
amorphous	having no shape
antidote	remedy for a poison
apathy	lack of interest or caring
arrogance	overconfidence
blueprint	a detailed outline or plan for a building
comprehensive	including everything, complete
condemn	to express strong disapproval of
conflagration	a widespread fire
conformity	the act of becoming similar or identical to
conventional	traditional, mundane
cynicism	the belief that all human action is motivated by selfishness
debunk	to expose the falseness
defendant	someone who has been accused of committing a crime
deliberate	*adj.* intentional, well thought out; *v.* to consider carefully
detrimental	causing damage or harm
divergent	moving in different directions from a common point
diversity	the state of being different or having different elements
dupe	a person easily deceived
elusive	cleverly avoiding or escaping
erratic	unpredictably eccentric
esoteric	known only by a select few
exacerbate	to make worse
exemplary	serving as an example; commendable
exploit	to take advantage of, to use selfishly for one's own ends
extraneous	not pertinent or relevant
fluid	capable of flowing; changing readily, as a plan
fundamental	basic, essential
ghastly	shockingly frightful
gullible	easily deceived
hiatus	a break or lapse in continuity
heir	a person who inherits another's belongings
hoard	to accumulate or stash away
implausible	not possible, not imaginable
impudence	bold disrespect or rudeness
inaudible	too quiet to be heard
incorrigible	not capable of being reformed
indecision	inability to decide

indelible	incapable of being erased
indifference	lack of interest, feeling, or opinion
indomitable	unable to be subdued or overcome
infallible	unable to be proven wrong
inferred	concluded by reasoning
ingenuity	cleverness; originality
injurious	causing damage or loss
innate	existing in a person since birth; part of the character of something
innocuous	causing or intending little or no harm
inquisitive	curious
integrity	honesty; moral uprightness
irrelevant	not necessary or important to the matter at hand
jargon	words used by people in a particular field of work
lamentation	an expression of sorrow or deep regret
lampoon	sharp satire
levity	lightness; lacking seriousness
lofty	having great height or a stately manner
lurid	gruesome, melodramatic, shocking
magnate	a person of great influence in a particular field
marred	impaired the perfection of
meager	lacking in amount or quality; poor
mediocrity	ordinariness, lack of distinction
methodical	orderly, having a set system
meticulous	very careful, attentive to details
migrate	to move from one place to another
miser	one who saves greedily
mitigate	to make less severe
mobility	ability to move or be moved
monarch	a ruler; a king, queen, or emperor
monotonous	boring; unvarying in tone or content
morose	gloomy; ill-tempered
mosaic	a picture made of small pieces of stone or glass
mundane	ordinary or commonplace
negate	to destroy the validity of something
novel	original, new and different
novice	a person who is new at something
nullify	to make invalid or worthless
obliterate	to wipe out, remove all traces
obscure	not known; difficult to understand
obsessive	overly preoccupied
objective	not affected by personal feelings
obsolete	outdated
ominous	signaling something evil is about to happen
omniscient	having complete knowledge

opaque	not transparent; hard to understand
paradox	something that seems to contradict itself
parochial	having a narrow scope
pastiche	piece of music, writing, or art combining several different sources or styles
patent	obvious, readily visible
paucity	small amount or number
penchant	a strong taste or liking
persecution	tormenting a person because of his or her beliefs
phenomena	occurrences, facts, or observable circumstances
philanthropist	someone who gives to worthy causes
phonetics	the study of sounds in a language
pioneer	*n.* a leader in a field; *v.* to lead the way in a field
pious	having reverence for a god
plagiarist	a person who presents someone else's work as his or her own
plateau	a condition of neither growth nor decline
precarious	unstable, insecure
preclude	to make impossible
predecessor	a person who precedes another in an office or a position
premonition	a feeling that something is about to happen
presumptuous	bold to the point of rudeness
prevailing	generally accepted; having superior power
prevalent	in general use or acceptance
prodigal	wasteful
prominent	standing out, important
promontory	a high point of land projecting into the sea
proposal	an offer or consideration or acceptance
provincial	having a narrow scope
provoke	anger, arouse, bring to action
purgation	the process of getting rid of impurities
quarry	a large open pit from which stone is cut
quibble	*v.* to make a minor objection; *n.* a small objection
raconteur	skilled storyteller
rebuttal	reply to a criticism or challenge
recant	to take back
recluse	someone who lives in seclusion
reconcile	to settle a problem
rectify	fix, correct
redundant	characterized by unnecessary repetition of words or ideas
reminiscence	a story of past experiences
regulate	to control or direct by some particular method
reign	*n.* having supreme power; *v.* to rule
reiteration	saying or doing something repeatedly
renounce	to give up or put aside
repeal	to take back a law or other decision

repertoire	supply of songs, stories, skills, or devices
replete	gorged with food, sated
repudiate	to cast off or disown; to refuse to acknowledge
residual	describing the part that is left over
resourceful	able to find solutions
resolute	strongly determined
reticent	untalkative, shy, reluctant to speak
retort	*v.* to reply sharply; *n.* a sharp reply
revere	to regard with awe
revelation	striking realization
rivalry	an ongoing competition
sanctuary	a safe place or a room for worship
sanction	*v.* to give permission; *n.* a coercive measure designed to make a person or persons comply
satiate	satisfy fully
sect	a subgroup of a religion; faction
sentinel	a guard, a watchman
serene	calm, peaceful
skeptical	showing doubt and disbelief
slander	untruthful spoken attack on someone's reputation
slothful	lazy
sluggish	lacking energy
sobriety	being quiet or serious
solidarity	fellowship between members of a group
solitude	the state of living or being alone
soporific	causing sleep
speculation	the act of thinking about or pondering something
spendthrift	a person who spends money wastefully
stanza	section of a poem
stimulus	something that causes a reaction
strident	harsh, grating
strive	try hard; make a major effort
stylized	in a particular style, often an unrealistic one
stoic	not affected by passion or feeling
stupefy	to make less alert
subdued	quiet, controlled, lacking in intensity
subordinate	placed in a lower order or rank
subtle	hardly noticeable
sullen	sad, sulky
succinct	brief, concise
succumb	to give way to superior force
superficial	near the surface; slight
superfluous	unnecessary
supremacy	the state of being supreme, or having the most power
surfeit	excess, overindulgence

suppleness	ability to bend easily; limberness
swindle	to cheat out of money or property
synopsis	plot summary
synthesis	the combining of separate parts to form a whole
symmetry	balanced proportions
synchronize	to cause to occur at the same time
synthesis	the combining of separate parts to form a whole
systematic	regular
tacit	implied, not stated outright
taciturn	being of few words
tactful	saying or doing the proper thing
taint	to affect with something harmful; contaminate
tantamount	equivalent in effect or meaning
taper	gradually decrease, grow smaller at one end; dwindle
temper	to moderate, to make less extreme
temperament	one's emotional nature
tenet	idea or belief
terminate	bring to an end
terrestrial	having to do with the earth
testimony	statement in support of something, often under oath
theologian	one who studies religion
theoretical	not proven true, existing only as an idea
thesis	unproven theory; long research paper
tirade	a long, harsh, often abusive speech
torpid	without energy, sluggish
tract	a piece of land
traitor	one who betrays a person, cause, or country
tranquillity	calmness, peacefulness
transcendent	going beyond known limits
trite	overused, lacking freshness
truant	someone who cuts school or neglects his or her duties
truncate	shorten by cutting off
tumultuous	characterized by a noisy uproar
unbiased	without prejudice
ubiquitous	being everywhere at the same time
unanimity	complete agreement
undermine	to injure or destroy underhandedly
unethical	having bad moral principles
unheralded	unnoticed or unappreciated
uniform	alike, identical
unnerving	upsetting; causing nervousness
unprecedented	without parallel
unseemly	unbecoming
unsound	not solid; not well founded; not healthy
unwitting	unaware

urbane	highly sophisticated
usurp	to seize power by force
utility	usefulness
vacillation	wavering; going back and forth
vagary	inconsistent or unpredictable action
vague	not precise; unclear
vane	a device that measures wind direction
vanquish	overpower an enemy completely
vegetation	plant life
veiled	covered or concealed
vengeful	wanting or seeking revenge
vent	express with emotion
verbosity	the use of too many words
uniform	alike, identical
verifiable	able to be proven true
versatile	capable of doing many things well
virtue	moral excellence
vigor	energy, vitality
vital	full of energy, necessary for life
vitality	energy, liveliness
vivid	sharp, intense, making an impression on the senses
vociferous	loud
void	to invalidate
vulnerable	capable of being hurt
wallow	to indulge in a particular state of mind
wariness	cautiousness
wharf	a structure built to extend from the land out over the water
whimsical	eccentric; unpredictable
wily	artful, cunning, deceitful, sly
witty	clever or amusing
wry	dryly humorous
yearning	a deep longing
zealous	very enthusiastic and intense

NOTES

NOTES

NOTES

NOTES

NOTES

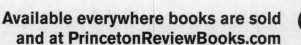